REACHING THE FAMILIES

A revision of the 1969 edition, this book takes the reader through the problems involved in beginning a service geared to non-churchgoing families. It explores ways in which the interest of both children and adults can be kept. There is a discussion of practical problems such as heating, lighting and sound. The sermon is covered in detail as are audio visual aids.

Michael Botting, at present Vicar of St George's, Leeds, is well known for his pioneering work in modern family services. He is joined in this edition by John Tigwell, an educationist, who is involved in Sunday School work at Scripture Union.

By the same author:

Teaching the Families

REACHING THE FAMILIES

MICHAEL BOTTING with JOHN TIGWELL

Falcon

First published 1969
New edition 1976
Copyright © Michael Botting 1969 and John Tigwell 1976
Biblical quotations unless otherwise stated are from
the Revised Standard Version (1946 and 1952)
ISBN 0 85491 837 X

FALCON BOOKS
are published by the Church Pastoral Aid Society,
Falcon Court, 32 Fleet Street, London EC4Y 1DB

Overseas Agents
EMU Book Agencies, 63 Berry Street,
Granville, 2142, NSW.
Scripture Union, PO Box 760,
Wellington, New Zealand
Sunday School Centre Wholesale, PO Box 3020,
Cape Town, South Africa
Anglican Book Society, 228 Bank Street,
Ottawa K2P 1XI, Canada

Made and printed in Great Britain by
Billing & Sons Ltd, Guildford, Surrey

Contents

Foreword

Even for the title alone I would be eager to commend this book to you, for I share Dr Coggan's view expressed within it that, for all the pressures which bear upon it in contemporary society, the family remains the setting in which the Gospel may be most readily learned and experienced. If this is so, we need hardly be surprised that, in Canon Craston's words, 'perhaps the only growing point in Church life today is the Family Service'. My experience in Liverpool would, I think, bear this out. I welcome, therefore, a book which deals in so practical a manner with the initiating and running of a regular Family Service, and is prepared to discuss the theological basis for this particular emphasis in our Church life.

I congratulate the authors and the publishers and wish this book, in its new edition, the success it deserves.

✠ *Stuart Ebor*
Bishopthorpe, York

Preface

Please read, preferably first, if you intend to attempt the other chapters that follow!

In our domestic and personal lives we are living in an age of disposable 'crockery' and throw-away handkerchiefs. Likewise in the Christian Church, and in the Church of England in particular, we are living in a period of throw-away books and disposable booklets. The first edition of *Reaching the Families* was to some extent out of date, as far as I was concerned, before it ever reached the bookshops. Six years after its publication parts of it are a positive embarrassment to me, so I am thankful it has now sold out and I have been asked to revise it, though I may be having similar trouble with this version before long. . . !

A number of things which have significantly affected this new edition are probably worth mentioning. For myself, just because of becoming an author of a book about Family Services, I have been invited to speak in a wide variety of places on this subject, and so have been able to benefit from other people's experience and appreciate better the complexity of many situations. I have also moved to a very different type of parish: geographically from south to north, and culturally from industrial to city centre (with a large eclectic congregation including students).

Then I have come to see that in attempting to evangelize the family and incorporate it into the total life of the church one has to give a lot more thought to the family itself. For that reason I have asked John Tigwell to join me as co-author. He is now Head Coordinator for Scripture Union and Secretary for Sunday Schools. He has also been a school teacher for 12 years. He has been involved in extensive research on the family as part of his work. Chapters or sections by John Tigwell are marked JT; otherwise it can be assumed that the chapters or sections are by me. For convenience, however, it has been found necessary to include most of this new material towards the end of the book.

In 1969 Family Services were comparatively rare, and were often little more than Mattins with a few choruses to replace a canticle, and a simplified sermon. Now Family Services seem to be springing up everywhere and have even been televised. Canon Colin Craston, writing in *The Churchman* (Winter 1971, page 269) refers to the phenomenon of Family Services 'perhaps the only widespread growing point in Church life'. If the sales of *Family Worship*[1] are anything to

[1] First published 1971 by the Church Pastoral Aid Society, Falcon Court, 32 Fleet Street, London EC4Y 1DB. Revised edition with new material 1975.

go by, Family Services are being introduced in many more parishes. Even diocesan authorities are known to be taking an interest in them. This means that this book must not only repeat some of the basic things for the benefit of those just starting Family Worship, but must also go much deeper for those who by now may have been in the 'game' for perhaps a decade, and feel their services need vitalizing. So I crave the patience of those readers who feel that in some places I state the obvious. When I was attempting to learn mathematics, my teachers often assumed that what was obvious to them was also obvious to me—but regrettably that was rarely the case!

In 1971 the Report *Christian Initiation: Birth and Growth in the Christian Society* (Chairman, The Bishop of Ely) was published by the Church of England Board of Education, and received by the General Synod of the Church of England at its York session in July of that year. Its contribution to family worship and evangelism will be obvious, but at the time of going to press it is still being debated. I hope my book will prove to anticipate some of the General Synod's decisions, but my gift of prophecy is limited and so my comments on page 78 will inevitably be tentative. I am extremely indebted to all the Diocesan Bishops and London Area Bishops who took the time and trouble to answer my questionnaire relating to children and the age of admission to Holy Communion.

I must point out that in *Teaching the Families* (Falcon 1973) various references are made by page number of chapter to sections of the First Edition of *Reaching the Families*. If the same page number applies to this revised version, that is purely coincidental, but every attempt has been made to ensure that all the information referred to has been repeated somewhere.

I gladly acknowledge my indebtedness to a number of people, and especially to Mary my wife who originally sparked off the idea of a Family Service in my mind and who encouraged me to persevere with it in spite of many obstacles. She also helped to sustain physically the various people who have come to our home to help with this and other publications relating to Family Services!

1 Thinking 'family'

1 How it all began

I first began thinking 'family' as a result of reading an article 'All right for the kids' in the *Church of England Newspaper* (6 October 1961).

'Religion is all right for women and kids.' 'You need religion to teach them right from wrong when they're young. Religion is kids' stuff.'

How did this idea arise in the minds of people? Certainly not from the New Testament. (I should think the verse 'Suffer the little children to come unto me' must be one of the most overworked texts in the gospel.) The Old Testament does not show an emphasis on youth either. There, children are usually thought of in relation to parents and family, which, in turn, is related to God.

The focus on young people has developed in the last 100 years or so. The Sunday School movement which began as an attempt to educate deprived children, has grown into a vast flood of organizations and activities for 'catching them young' for the Church.

Various half-truths in the heads of devoted Christians have helped the process. The RCs say 'Give us a child until it is seven, and we'll make it an RC for life.' The RC Church today is probably too astute not to have learnt the lesson of her lapsed. 'The child of today is the Church of tomorrow. Therefore we must go flat out on youth clubs, uniformed organizations, Bible classes and Sunday schools, and the staffs to run them.' If this theory were even half true, the churches of the larger parishes, with hundreds on their Sunday school registers, should now be having an accommodation problem for adults in their churches.

This described my experience exactly. As vicar of my first living, I had inherited a situation in which the Sunday School had obviously been very large and successful, but whose present losses vastly outstripped the intake. Furthermore, I was frequently discovering that couples coming to see me about getting married or having their baby christened used to be in the Sunday School or one of the youth organizations. My thoughts, which eventually had to be put into words, were that the real success or lack of success of the Sunday School was seen not in the numbers of children who had come in the past, but in the number of adults now forming the real core of the parish's workers. Of such success, there was very little evidence.

Not unnaturally, the Sunday School teachers were somewhat distressed to think that much of their work, extending in some cases over a quarter of a century, appeared to have been largely a waste of time. Of course, this was too sweeping a statement, for we know that

God's word will not return to Him empty, but accomplish His
purpose (Isaiah 55.11). There must have been, and perhaps still is, a
significant amount of reaping going on among adults as a direct
result of sowing in Sunday School in earlier days. Jesus confirms the
saying, 'One sows and another reaps. I sent you to reap that for which
you did not labour; others have laboured, and you have entered into
their labour' (John 4.37-38).

However, it was one thing to see what was wrong but quite another
to see the solution. This same article in the *CEN* gave me a clue:

The Jehovah's Witnesses are probably the best example of growth.
I asked one of them in a local factory what they do about Sunday
Schools. He looked at me oddly and said, 'We don't have them.
They have no scriptural precedent.' He said that from Moses onwards
parents brought their children with them for instruction, and the
JWs followed that example.

'From Moses onwards parents brought their children with them for
instruction.' Here was the clue. What we needed was some form of
service specially geared to suit the whole family.

This idea was strengthened by several further factors. Firstly I read
in the correspondence columns of the *CEN* (13 October 1961):

'I write in strong commendation of your correspondent's views
in "All right for the kids".

'Over the past 50 years the range and number of organizations
dealing with young people's evangelism have increased enormously.
Many of these organizations are so much part of the religious scene
that their *raison d'être* is never examined. Sufficient justification seems
to be found in the fact that there are spiritual "results" without consideration of what percentage of the results are really lasting. Little
is said and written on the theological principles involved in children's
work.

'We have, as your correspondent points out, waited several decades
for the great influx of adults we have been promised on the basis of
the accepted "catch 'em young" assumption—the argument usually
unearthed whenever any criticism disturbs the steady drive for help
with classes, clubs, camps, etc.

'If our work of evangelism were concerned merely with overcoming
a sort of "sales resistance" which increased with age, all well and good.
This would indeed necessitate mental conditioning as early as possible.
But children born in sin are by nature as hostile to the gospel as adults,
although this antipathy may be shown in different ways. All ages

need a sovereign work of God the Holy Ghost to bring them to new birth. There is no difference. The gospel is the power of God to everyone who believes.'

The reason that children left the Sunday School at about 12 years old and were not seen again until their wedding, seemed to be that, like their parents, they were hostile to the gospel, and if not soundly converted before 12 years of age would stop going to church because it was a sign of growing up. 'Dad doesn't go, so why should I?'

But supposing Dad did go, had been going for some years, had received Jesus Christ as his Saviour, and was seeking to bring others to share that experience: what would then be the attitude of the 12-year-old? Despite his possible rebellion, natural at that age, would it not seem logical to join the Bible class for teenagers with the active encouragement of parents, rather than the more usual direct or indirect discouragement, and quite apart from the inclination to watch some interesting programme on television or attend the local swimming baths?

The second factor to strengthen my idea of a Family Service came from some remarks made by Dr Coggan, then Archbishop of York, in his Presidential Address to the Convocation of York in 1962. He spoke of the danger of alienating and dividing families rather than uniting them:

'I detect a dangerous tendency in our present Church "set-up" to defeat the very end towards which we are working. The end is quite clear in our minds—the creation of strong, loyal, instructed, witnessing Christian families. But are the means that we use best suited to the achievement of that end? Is not some of the "departmentalizing" of our church work inimical to that end? I am all for the Mothers' Union, the Church of England Men's Society, the Girls' Friendly Society, the Young Men's Class, and so on. But when all these departmentalized activities flourish most, should we not at least ask ourselves whether there is not a danger of our *dividing* the family rather than *uniting* it in Christian discipleship, training, and even worship? Is it possible that we, who believe so profoundly in the institution of the Christian family, and who speak often and vehemently about it, are, by the very form which our church work takes, not helping—perhaps are even hindering—that for which we stand? A move in the right direction has been made in many churches where, the Sunday School having proved in a particular neighbourhood an unsuitable method of instructing the young, "family church" has taken its place, and after corporate family worship, the children have left their parents for separate instruction only to join them at the end of the service. I suspect that this method, with suitable local variations, is capable of considerable extension. Let us take a fresh look at the shape of our church life and organizations. Let us ask ourselves whether our church families might not do more *together*.'

This view was further strengthened by writers of other denominations. For example, Abbé Michonneau in his book *Revolution in a City Parish* (Blackfriars, 1949) states:

'We have stopped clubs at Colombes . . . we lean too heavily on parish activities, and especially on those dealing with children, in our attempts to advance the kingdom of God. We work with children too much, and not enough with families. A child is yet to be formed; he is plastic. More often than not it is his anti-Christian family which has the preponderant influence upon him' (pages 58, 69).

'Is it our job, as priests, to amuse children and keep adolescents occupied? Our task is one of conversion, preaching, education, distributing the Sacraments. If the children are in the gutters, so are the adults, and in a more harmful manner. While we are trying to keep the youngsters happy, their father is in a bar-room, their mother in a cinema, and their elder sisters and brothers God knows where. Certainly it is a shame to see children being neglected, but it is still worse to see adults being ruined, families being de-christianized. It is better for us to bring them to Christ directly' (pages 57ff.).[1]

Lastly, my views on Family Services arose very naturally from the Baptism policy I was just beginning to develop. It seemed to me from Scripture that the Baptism of infants was only really justified where at least one parent was a practising Christian. I realized that it would be invidious for me to judge who was a Christian and who was not, but felt a reasonable case could be made for expecting regular worship and full church membership.

But even to start getting parents back to church was going to be impossible, humanly speaking, with the Sunday service pattern as it then was at our church. Of the three services we held on a Sunday (Holy Communion at 8.00 am, Morning Prayer at 11.00 am, and Evening Prayer at 6.30 pm), the only possibility for parents of young children was Morning Prayer. Yet it seemed to me that there would

[1] Quoted from *What is Evangelism?* by Canon Douglas Webster (Highway Press, 1959) page 18.

have to be many changes in that service if those parents who did occasionally come to church were going to want to come back week by week.

Apart from weddings and christenings, in which there were other interests, the services had very little in common with either their everyday life or their previous experience of church, when and if they had come to Sunday School. There were more pews empty than occupied, and everyone except them seemed to know what was supposed to be happening, so that they felt 'odd men out', the *Te Deum* droned on for ages and the tunes would never have been considered for the 'pop' charts. The sermon lasted at least 20 minutes and the preacher frequently used words which, though found in the Bible, were not normally used in everyday life.

Yet, had they only realized it, the vicar was preaching the much-emphasized expository sermon, and it would have been his concern that before he left the parish the 'whole counsel of God' should have been declared.

On top of all this, these brave new worshippers had to face the jibe on the way home, 'Think you are better than us, do you? We saw you going to church', and the episode might well end with a row between husband and wife because the Sunday lunch was not ready on time!

The jibes from the neighbours we could and should not attempt to avoid. It is bound to be part of the cost of the witness of attending public worship. But I felt the parish, under the leadership of the vicar and the Parochial Church Council, should take active steps to produce a form of Family Service as an evangelistic bridge to the entirely unchurched, only some of whom might have had Sunday School training. This is what seemed to be needed in my parish, and I have come to believe that this is what is needed in most, if not all, of the parishes of our land.

I know it is said that one can prove anything with statistics, and some people use them as a drunken man uses a lamp-post, more for support than illumination. Nevertheless, I found the following completely independent sets of figures most significant:

Statistics which were kept between the first and second world wars at one particular Anglican church showed that of children *sent* to Sunday School only 2½% stayed and became active adult church members, whereas of children *brought* to church with their parents 96% stayed.

In No. 7 of *Christians in Industrial Areas* George Venables writes of a

Brethren Assembly in Stafford: 'Between the years 1919 and 1939, over 1000 children passed through our Sunday School, and more than 350 professed conversion at six children's missions, three conducted by the late R. Hudson Pope. All the children of church members who passed through the school became church members, though several had lost all interest when they returned from the 1939–1945 war and some joined other churches. Only $2\frac{1}{2}\%$ of the Sunday School children from non-Christian homes became church members and all those had contacts with Christian homes or Covenanters during their teens.'

Every church inevitably has limited physical resources, therefore it must use the man and woman power it has to the maximum extent. Who could tell how much more effective our work would be if instead of going all out for children we majored on adults, especially parents?

Another frequent justification for the emphasis on Sunday School work is based on the verse, 'a little child shall lead them' (Isaiah 11.6) This has been interpreted as meaning that we aim to reach the parents through the children. But my reading of that text says nothing about parents, but rather of the wolf, the lamb, the leopard and the kid; furthermore, this passage is hardly concerned with evangelistic opportunities, for the earth is there described as 'full of the knowledge of the Lord as the waters cover the sea' (verse 9).

We must therefore get right away from the unbiblical idea that parents, or any adults for that matter, should necessarily be reached for the Lord by means of the children. Of course, some parents have been won that way just as some children, despite the strongest opposition from home, have been retained by the Church after the age when the majority of children tend to fall away. I once heard of a woman who fell down a well and this led directly to her conversion; but no one would deliberately leave covers off wells in the remote chance that those who fell down them should become converted!

God's basic unit is the family,[1] therefore we should hardly be surprised to find in the Bible that God's method of reaching the children is through the parents.

'. . . that this my be a sign among you, when your children ask in time to come, "What do these stones mean to you?" Then you shall tell them that the waters of the Jordan were cut off before the ark of the

[1] See page 13 where John Tigwell writes more fully on the family as God's basic unit.

covenant of the Lord; when it passed over the Jordan, the waters of the Jordan were cut off. So these stones shall be to the people of Israel a memorial for ever' (Joshua 4.6–7[1]).

I therefore believe that we should cater for the family as a whole at least once in our Sunday pattern of church worship.

2 The Family Service

As far back as 1958 Canon G. R. Sainsbury pointed out to the Church Assembly that there had been a tendency to underestimate the real importance of the family in the ordinary man's life. Whatever job he may be in, he is also a family man, and it is in the setting of the family that he is most sensitive to special influences.

After all, most of us eat together as a family, watch TV together, go on holiday together; therefore surely the greatest and most natural thing that we should do together as a family is to worship God, who set us together in families. There seems to be much to be gained from the 'togetherness' of the family in the context of family worship.

A Family Service, then, is a service designed to speak to all the family at the same time. While it is deliberately made simple and probably shorter than other services, it is not only for the children. Such names as 'Children's Church' or 'Young people's Service' do not describe it, because the service is just as much, if not more, for adults as for children.

I would therefore take issue with Canon Michael Hocking in his *A handbook of Parish Work* (Mowbrays, 1974) when he writes of a Family Service as 'meant chiefly for children, but which also brings in their parents' (page 66). I naturally agree with him where he advises the new incumbent not to stop a Family Service and put much thought into it. However, I would seriously question the extent to which children are used to undertake tasks in the service which would normally be expected to be done by adults (page 88).

A more exact description of a Family Service becomes difficult, firstly because situations vary considerably from parish to parish. In some parishes church-going may be the 'done thing', and most people will have been confirmed at school as a matter of course. For them a simple type of Family Service may be satisfactory, say once a month, but something more mature may be needed on other

[1] See also Psalm 78.1–8; Mark 10.13; John 4.53; Acts 16.30–34; Ephesians 6.1–4; 2 Timothy 3.15 with 1.5.

Sundays, without losing the family orientation of the family instruction and worship. More is written about this in chapter 4. In other parishes church-going may not only *not* be the 'done thing' but something to be steadily resisted, and, as for 'Confirmation', it is a meaningless term.

Because every parish is different, the recommendations in this book will have to be modified and adapted to each situation. It needs to be remembered that the majority of parishes in this country are predominantly 'working class' (like the one in which I started my Family Services, and similar to part of my present one), where it is very much more difficult to get people to come to church and to consider the gospel than it is in middle or upper class parishes. However, it was interesting that at the Study Conference on Evangelism at Morecambe in 1972 the first edition of *Reaching the Families* was required reading for those working in *suburban* parishes. In *Teaching the Families* I quoted a vicar who wrote to tell me that his Family Services were founded very much on *Reaching the Families* lines, and said, 'It has caused a revolution here! We have a full church every Sunday morning, and have been able to get a curate on the strength of all the follow-up work that has resulted.' That also was referring to a *suburban* area.

A further difficulty is that the purpose of starting a Family Service may not be the reason for its continuance later on. I can best explain this by means of an illustration from my previous parish. My purpose in starting a Family Service was quite deliberately and unashamedly to reach men and women, especially parents; but I knew that I had to tell Bible stories and talk to them in terms suitable for children of 12 years old, because in most cases that was the age when these adults' religious knowledge had stopped, being the age at which they left Sunday School. I needed therefore to have children of that age present at the service. The 12-year-old children needed this teaching in the service as part of the normal Sunday School curriculum; but I also needed to have them present so that I could talk to them and the adults at the same time without the latter feeling that they were being talked down to or patronized. That this system was the correct one to adopt I have no doubt, for there are converted parents in that church today whose way back to God began through Family Service. It was there that they began to realize they were not Christians as they had originally thought.

However, later the situation arose where converted parents continued to come, not primarily for themselves, although they would be the first to admit that God could still speak to them through this simple type of service, but because they wanted to set their children an example and so help them to continue going to church during their teens. Such parents are now confirmed and share in other services on a Sunday where the teaching is of 'stronger meat'.

To summarize, a Family Service rightly understood is a service geared to the whole family, so that the basic worshipping unit in the church is not the young people or the children, but God's unit, the family. It needs to be grasped that, in the early years, the main purpose for the service may be to get the adults into the church, while an additional reason for its perpetuation may be to keep the children, that they might grow into mature, practising, adult Christians.

Inevitably this book is specialized in the sense that it is written for those with some degree of leadership in local churches. We hope and pray that readers in a position to do so will be helped and encouraged to make the worship and evangelism in the parish *family orientated*, because they have become convinced, as we have, that this is a thoroughly biblical means of bringing the gospel of Jesus Christ effectively to every man's door, and bringing whole families into the worship and life of the local church.

3 The Family—God's basic unit (JT)

It was God's intention from the beginning that family should not be just a 'dynasty' related by flesh and blood, but a meaningful and growing relationship, firstly between husband and wife and then blossoming out through children. As we study the first two chapters of Genesis we notice that God made woman not essentially that man might reproduce but because it was not good for man to be alone. 'Then the Lord God said, "It is not good that the man should be alone; I will make him a helper fit for him" ' (Genesis 2.18). It is to make this lasting relationship of love and sharing that man and woman are called to leave mother and father and become one flesh (2.24).

In his book *I married you* (IVP) Walter Trobisch explores at great depth the meaning of this 'leaving' and 'cleaving'. All we need to say here is that it is the relationship between man and woman that is the key to our understanding of the family as God's basic unit in society. Unless man and woman break the physical and intimate ties that bind them to their parents and make a deeply physical and intimate relationship with one another, no lasting relationship can be formed and no meaningful family life established. A person's relationship with mother and father can never be the same after marriage, however harmonious this relationship is, for the physical and intimate tie which bound them is for ever broken.

Some people say that today's 'family' of father, mother and children is not God's pattern. This small unit of the immediate family is often called the 'nuclear' family. It is suggested that if we returned to a so-called biblical pattern of family structure, great-grandparents, grandparents, parents, children, aunts, uncles, slaves, servants, etc., would all have to be included, all living in close proximity; this would then provide us with a solution to the difficulties our nuclear families experience in their relationship with one another. However, is such an alternative structure biblical at all? Genesis 2.18 is explicit in its injunction to man and woman to give themselves exclusively to each other, and there seems little evidence from Scripture that, for example, Jacob did not retain his own household and his sons their households mutually independent as far as the intimacies of each family's relationships with one another were concerned.

As we consider the biblical concept of Family, we find so often that Scripture is far more concerned about relationships than about structures, though it is true that the Bible does speak about structures in the family and this must be considered later. Throughout Scripture God is depicted as Father of His children (Psalm 89.26, Isaiah 64.8), and the characteristics of the Father's relationship with His children are the basic characteristics to be found in the relationships within the human family. The more I study the relationship of God with His children, the more I realize that what God says in His word about structures in society, in the world, in nations, in churches and in families, depends first and foremost on my understanding of His relationship with me as my heavenly Father.

God trusts His children, and His relationship with them is a relationship of trust even though He *knows* that they will betray His trust. God made a covenant with Abraham even though Abraham had already failed Him. God had, as it were, no evidence that He could trust Abraham, but He did trust him with His eternal covenant. So it was with Noah the father of rebellious sons, Moses the murderer, David the adulterer and the apostles who betrayed God's son and left Him to face the last hours alone. We speak a great deal of our need to trust God, and this is right, but we often neglect the most forceful part of God's relationship with man as our heavenly Father—that He trusts us. Trust should be the pre-eminent relationship within God's family, and therefore as God Himself has chosen the father–child analogy, so it must be of first importance within the human family.

God, however, does not just trust us His children with His covenant of grace to man, but God loves His children unconditionally. God did not withdraw His love for Israel even when Israel was faithless and disobedient. Israel then lost the benefits of that love, but God still loved. 'It was not because you were more in number than any other people that the Lord set his love upon you and chose you, for you were the fewest of all peoples; but it is because the Lord loves you' (Deuteronomy 7.7–8a); 'I have loved you with an everlasting love; therefore I have continued my faithfulness to you' (Jeremiah 31.3).

This relationship of unconditional love is part of the character of God. 'God is love', and this characteristic of love is demanded by God in His children and thus by God in the basic unit of society, the family. 'As the Father has loved me, so have I loved you; abide in my love' (John 15.9). 'I command you to love one another' (John 15.17). If God's love, pre-eminently shown in Jesus, is unconditional, then God's people with whom He is related will only discover their own identity and fulfilment in life when their own interpersonal relationships are carried out in the spirit of unconditional love.

It is against this background of relationships within the family that we can study the biblical structures of family.

(a) The essence of the family

The family is the basic unit of society and stems from God's creating work (Genesis 2.18–25). The fall of man has resulted in its created purpose of unity and harmony having been broken (Genesis 3.16). However, the purpose of the Creator has not been entirely destroyed, for man is still made after the image of God. Therefore, although perfect harmony and unity cannot exist in families outside the redeeming grace of God, nevertheless all human families bear in some part the mark of their Creator's purpose.

Ephesians 5.22–6.4 remind us of God's structure for families: father–mother–children, an exclusive and interdependent unit.

(b) Individual roles within the family

Ephesians 5.25 says, 'Husbands, love your wives, as Christ loved the church and gave himself up for her.' The husband is called by God to be the head of his family and bear responsibility for it both materially and spiritually. He is to love and give himself up for his wife as Christ did the church. Some have seen here in Ephesians the picture of the dominating husband commanding unthinking obedience from his wife in some strange Victorian manner. This is surely a completely unthinkable relationship, and totally contrary to what we have already learnt of God's teaching on relationship, trust, and unconditional love. Indeed, how does Christ love the Church, the pattern a husband is to copy in his relationship with his wife? Is He domineering, autocratic, dictatorial, unmindful of the personality or needs of the individual members of His Church? Surely not! Christ loved His Church in a self-sacrificial way, forgiving, forgetting, restoring, caring, giving abundantly more than ever the Church dreamed of. So husbands are commanded to love their wives as Christ loved His Church.

The husband is also expected to exercise his priesthood within the family as the one who teaches his children and passes on to them the living faith (Ephesians 6.4). He is expected also to be the one on whom the ultimate responsibility for the fair disciplining of the children rests. We may note, however, that although the ultimate authority rests in the father, discipline rests clearly as a shared responsibility of both mother and father. 'Children, obey your parents in everything, for this pleases the Lord' (Colossians 3.20).

'Wives, be subject to your husbands as to the Lord' (Ephesians 5.22). The wife is called to obey her husband and share in the care and nurture of children. However, we must not forget what we have already learnt about our relationships in the family, our unconditional love for one another, and also what Paul said in Galatians 3.28. God's word does not contradict itself. In Ephesians Paul is speaking of the function or role of husband and wife, not of their status; our status is that before God there is neither male nor female, but we are 'all one in Christ Jesus'.

Children are to honour and obey their parents (Colossians 3.20, see Ephesians 6.1-4). Parents must note the caution that they are not to provoke their children to anger. How often is the rebellion and disobedience of the child attributable to the provocation of the parent? Our desire is that our children will learn from us as parents the wonderful grace of our God. To learn about God the Father the child looks to his own father. Does he find in us a trust and unconditional love similar to what we find in our heavenly Father? Does he find in his family that relationship of love we urge him to find in the family of God? This frightening responsibility to nurture our children in the faith is part of the discipline we are called as parents to exercise within our homes. It is this caring, compassionate love that brings the honour and obedience from our children of which the Scripture speaks. Parents need to remember, however, as we see our children develop

and mature, that ultimately the 'break' and 'make' that initiated our
own family will take that family from us to 'make' anew and to cleave
to another. More than this, if the nurture and care 'in the Lord' that
our home provides has any meaning, then our children must learn a
higher and greater love and allegiance. 'He who loves father or mother
more than me is not worthy of me . . .' (Matthew 10.37).

(c) The role of the family

It is difficult in examining the teaching of God's Word on 'family'
to separate the distinctive function of the family from the function of
the Church as family. There is a particular sense in which the family is
to reflect in its relationships, in its actions and in its priorities those
relationships, actions and priorities which are commanded for the
whole Church. But the family is particularly to be a reproductive unit
(Genesis 1.18), a sanctuary into which newly created life may be
brought and in which the living faith is passed to the next generation
(Deuteronomy 4.9, see the warning of Judges 2.10).

As we explore in this book ways in which we might reach families
with the gospel, we need to reflect on God's purpose for the family,
and realize that what we do and what we say should lead families
together into meaningful relationships with one another and with
their God. Our church structures, our demands on time and our
method of work should at all times encourage and commend the
biblical qualities of family life which we have now briefly considered.

2 Starting a Family Service

1 Preliminary preparation

Prayer

Like everything else done in the Lord's name and for His sake, organizing a Family Service should begin with prayer. We know that without the Lord's blessing we can do nothing.

Because the service is especially designed to be a long-term, concentrated evangelistic project, attacking the devil's domain—the unchurched world—there is going to be opposition. Unfortunately, some of this opposition may come from the most unexpected sources, namely, the very people who might be expected to be especially concerned with evangelism. Starting a Family Service, therefore, will begin as a topic for the prayers of the vicar or minister, and it should be shared with the leaders of the church and all who can be relied upon to pray regularly.

Counting the cost

The cost to be counted is not primarily in pounds and pence. In terms of money, it is very difficult to say how much a Family Service costs. Each expense has to be faced as it comes, and more will be said about that at the appropriate moment. In counting the cost I am thinking of other factors.

Firstly, the cost to the vicar or minister. The Family Service should never be automatically delegated to the assistant curate, if the parish has one. Indeed, there are various reasons why, in an ordinary parish, it should be seen to be the vicar's special 'baby' to which he brings all his past parochial experience (however limited that may be). For example, he must face the fact that he may have to give an original talk, suitable for quite a wide range including children, most Sundays of the year, with an especially good one at the most difficult times such as Christmas, Easter and Harvest. It is my personal view, even though I have been brought up in circles where talks to adults and children were quite often required, that this sort of address, though shorter to deliver, takes far longer and is far more difficult to prepare than a sermon for adults only.

There are other reasons why Family Service should be the vicar's responsibility. He is more likely than the curate to be a family man himself. He is likely to stay in the parish longer than any curate, and in a long-term venture such as this, continuity of leadership is vital. Further, as has been inferred already, there may be difficulties to face within the church as a whole. It is better that the vicar deals with these directly, with the tact that longer experience in the ministry brings, rather than having to sort out a difficult situation on behalf of his curate.

Then there is the cost to the parish. Many parishes which would vote Labour almost to a man in an election are strictly conservative when parochial changes are envisaged! This has to be overcome. It has to be pointed out, gently but none the less firmly, that pagans and their children come first, and Christians and their Sunday lunch last, when planning an evangelistic service. The importance of this factor will become obvious later in this chapter. The congregation will be called upon to provide a lot of helpers to do various jobs every week for most of the year, and the jobs will not always be very attractive. (Dealing with someone else's baby who has been sick in the crèche just at the beginning of the sermon is no pleasant task!)

One further comment before we proceed: we should never despise 'the day of small things' (Zechariah 4.10). My first Family Service[1] began with the astonishing total of 32, almost all of whom I knew personally, despite extensive visiting and many promises by non-churchgoers that they would be there. In fact, the icy chills of the hardest winter for many years reduced my Family Service on one occasion to a Family Service indeed—my own family, just the four of us!

What time should the service be held?
After considerable discussion with many people in my previous parish, we decided on 10 am. I have been interested to notice in correspondence with some 40 parishes holding Family Services, that 10 am is overwhelmingly the most popular time.

From the point of view of those with young families, they will be able to have a 'lie-in' when the service is at this time. Further, as it should not last more than three-quarters of an hour and may take less, most families who live in the average-sized parish and walk to church, could be home by 11 am so that they still have two hours to prepare the Sunday lunch. At this point, Christians must beware of being 'pi' and saying that this should not be a consideration. For these recently

[1] I should perhaps explain that the planning of the Family Service described in this book is not exactly what I did myself, but what I should have done had I known when I started what I now know. Originally, Family Service began at 10, but as an 'extra' to the other services of the day, and not combined with Sunday School.

non–churchgoing families, the Sunday lunch *is* a consideration, and not until they are converted can we expect it to be otherwise. Of course, when there are very young babies in the family who have fixed feeding times, or where the father is on shift work, there will be no time of day that will regularly be convenient for everyone.

From the point of view of the parish, 10 am still enables other morning services to be fitted in without undue overcrowding. For instance, there can still be an 8 am celebration, and/or full Morning Prayer at 11 or 11.15. *The Prayer Book (Alternative and Other Services) Measure* 1965 enables the minister, with the agreement of the Parochial Church Council, to replace (say) Morning Prayer with a Family Service, so that on a normal Sunday morning the pattern might be Family Service at 10 am and full Communion Service at 11.15.

Alternatively, Family Service can be regarded as the ministry of the word and prayer section of either Series 2 or 3, so after a short break to allow those who do not wish to stay to leave (or to have coffee), the latter half of the Holy Communion Service can proceed. If the crèche is allowed to continue and the Sunday School children can be looked after by Sunday School teachers, the arrangement can be a great help to enable parents to receive Holy Communion together. This part of the Communion Service need not last more than half an hour at the very most. If this arrangement is difficult every week, it can be done, say, fortnightly, or monthly. See also chapters 4 and 5.

Of course in some parishes 10 am may be a hopeless time, my present parish being one. However, in selecting a better time there seem to be several very good reasons against holding it in the afternoon.

Firstly, it is not the best time of the day for the teachers to feel their best for teaching, nor would their classes be able to attend so easily, especially if there had been a heavy Sunday dinner. Secondly, there has been the tendency to go out in the family car. Thirdly, teachers themselves will welcome an afternoon's rest on the very day that is, after all, the Christian Sabbath.

How often should the service be held?
Should Family Services be held weekly, fortnightly or monthly? If the full implications and purpose of Family Services have been grasped, I do not really believe there is any choice. Family-orientated worship should be a weekly event like any other of our Sunday services. If we want to encourage weekly attendance at the Lord's House, we must surely start in that way. To some prospective worship-

pers, this may seem an impossible ideal, but even if they, in fact, only start coming monthly, or fortnightly, it does not harm to have the goal of weekly attendance constantly before them.

From the minister's point of view when visiting, it is very much easier to say to a family 'Come to Family Service next Sunday', than to say 'Come to our Family Service—but let me see, when is the next one? Oh yes, in three weeks' time.' It is much easier to forget an engagement, however seriously a person may intend to keep it, when it is in three weeks' time, than when it is in a matter of a few days, particularly in areas where people do not keep diaries. Besides, if it is every month or every fortnight, there is always the confusion that is caused when there is a five-Sunday month.

Finally there is the problem of shift work. Many men living in industrial areas do shift work on a two or three week basis. This can mean in terms of church attendance that two or even three Sundays in the month can be ruled out. Anything less than a weekly Family Service is useless to such people.

In some parishes where the whole idea of a Family Service is strongly resisted, it might be wise to start by having one monthly to give people some idea of what to expect. When people discover that Family Services attract conspicuously larger congregations, they may soon be persuaded to accept them weekly.

Where should the service be held?
Here again, under normal circumstances there seems to be no choice. Family Service is an important occasion and demands red carpet treatment in the parish church. There must be no suggestion that Family Service could be held, for example, in the parish hall. Family Service is a service in its own right like Holy Communion or Evening Prayer, and must be seen to be so. Besides, as it is designed to make adults and children regular worshippers, it should start where we want them to continue. Of course, in some situations there may be a daughter church or chapel-of-ease where the Family Service could be held with no loss of prestige. Under those circumstances it could be a positive gain, for families could come to see this as their church in a special way. A daughter church may be on a new housing estate, just where most of the families actually live, and so would be much more convenient than dragging them far down into the more central part of the town.

The main point is that unless circumstances are particularly unusual, the Family Service should take place in a consecrated building.

My own present circumstances are making me have to eat my own words, to some extent. There is a distinct cultural gap between the working class parish and my city centre church with its 'eclectic' congregation on which the church is, humanly speaking, substantially dependent to maintain the widely known crypt work. Consequently we are attempting to discover some suitable venue very much closer to those living in the parish than is the church itself, preferably some place that parents and children are used to frequenting. A church school would be ideal, but there is not one central enough. I mention this to illustrate that one's plans for a Family Service have to be flexible.

The bishop

There are a couple of reasons why I believe Anglican clergy should keep their local bishop informed about Family Service plans by letter, a personal visit, or a serious chat after some episcopal occasion. Firstly, he will be interested to know what is going on in his area, and will only be able to pray intelligently if he is kept informed on all matters.

The other reason is that, as I have already indicated, some parishioners seem to dislike change, however necessary and long overdue it may be. There is always the chance that someone unsympathetic to the Family Service may write to the bishop without the vicar's knowledge, and the true facts of what is being planned may not tally exactly with what the bishop is told. If he knows what you are doing he will be in a better position to reply to such letters, and may well be able to add a word of support for the changes.

The Parochial Church Council

If the vicar does not have the PCC right behind him in a venture of this sort, his task is going to be difficult indeed, for the PCC can help to remould the thinking of the whole parish, and comprises, after all, the parishioners' elected representatives.[1] This is even more the case in the free churches, with the Deacons or Elders system. At some time or another, the Family Service should be placed on the agenda. It may be valuable to circulate Council members with an outline of what is in mind, so that there is plenty of time to think and pray about it before the matter is discussed at the meeting. In this way,

[1] Besides, the Prayer Book (Alternative and Other Services) Measure 1965 requires the agreement of the PCC before the minister may introduce into the parish church any experimental services.

any less helpful suggestions which might have been made on the spur of the moment will never be aired, and will not therefore have to be retracted. Here is the sort of circular letter I have in mind.

The Nature and Times of Church Services at the Parish Church
Please note that in raising this matter, it is not my intention to make any changes whatever without real evidence that they are desirable, hence my asking for them to be discussed by the PCC.

Secondly, should we decide on any changes, they would not be put into operation until the whole parish had been circularized well in advance; and even then it might be wise to have them for a trial period and discuss them again in the light of experience.

It seems desirable that in deciding what services we should hold, provided we obey statutory regulations, we should ensure the following:

1 Services for all stages of Christian growth
2 Services for all physical ages
3 Least duplication of services.

It will be appreciated that the more talks and sermons the clergy have to prepare, the less time they can give to each.

When I sent a circular letter of this sort, I suggested some possibilities as to arrangement of services, none of which we adopted, because a PCC member made a much better suggestion. The result was that the decision to change the times of our services and make Family Service a service in its own right was unanimously agreed in one and a quarter hours. I have not been aware of any regular churchgoer who has regretted the day we made the change. I personally visited the one or two people who only attended the early Holy Communion Service, which we were dropping, and explained the reason for the change, persuading them to see that it was for the general good of the parish and the spread of the Gospel that such a change should be made.

The Sunday School
In a booklet *Reaching and Teaching the Children*, published some years ago and now out of print, Canon Liddle Paine gave the following reasons why Sunday School ought not to be abandoned:

(a) With the intimacy and informality of a Sunday School, there is the unequalled opportunity of personal contact with the children in the teaching periods, as well as on other occasions. In Sunday School, the spirit-filled teacher can really and sympathetically get to know his children.

(b)   In the Church today, there are still many strong advocates of Scripture memorization. Despite the difficulty of coaxing the modern child to 'learn his text', many portions of God's Word are being committed to memory through the agency of our Sunday Schools. Who can doubt that this will bear fruit?

(c)   Particularly in the primary Sunday Schools, there is the opportunity for activity and expression work. Furthermore, in all departments, there is a place for the question-and-answer technique of imparting knowledge. All this can be done more effectively in the informal atmosphere of a Sunday School.

(d)   In the efficiently conducted Sunday School, constant contact is maintained with the parents. This is done through periodic parents' meetings and by the visitation of the homes of the children on the part of the teachers. In the case of the primary Sunday School, very often the parents are seen both before and after the Sunday School session.

(e)   The Sunday School gives the opportunity for consecutive instruction. Thus the children are provided with a fairly comprehensive groundwork of Bible knowledge. (The teachers themselves, incidentally, stand to improve enormously their knowledge of God's Word).

(f)   There is a distinct advantage in the age-groupings which obtain in most of our Sunday Schools. Instruction suitable to each grade is given. Furthermore, the top classes proceed to the separate Youth Groups, which may be Covenanters, Pathfinders, or some other body. Ideally, these sections should produce the trainee teachers.

While Canon Paine and I envisage a rather different concept of Family Service, I quote him because I agree with all he says concerning Sunday School, although I see no reason why it should not be combined with the morning Family Service. As I have already indicated, I believe there are good reasons for avoiding church activities on a Sunday afternoon; yet the Sunday School method has much of value which must not be lost.

If there has been an old-fashioned Sunday School that teachers are reluctant to relinquish, they should be shown gradually that, if there is hall space close to the church so that children could easily leave the main worship area during the Family Service, the teachers will not be losing their job. In my previous parish we had a crèche for babies up to three years old, nursery Sunday School for three- to five-year-olds, and primary Sunday School from five to seven years. All these normally met in their own separate rooms, although some came into church on very special occasions such as Christmas.

The junior and senior Sunday Schools (8–11 years old) came into church every Sunday, the former leaving during the middle of the service for their own talk, while the adults and the seniors of the Sunday School remained in church for the entire service. These seniors, who were between the ages of 11–12 years old, were in the top class of the Sunday School and would the following year move up into Bible classes. They sat in church with the teachers they had had in their previous year in Sunday School. The presence of this group was helpful because it gave a reason for the talk being fairly simple without the adults being given the impression they were 'being talked down to'.

However, over the course of time we found some of senior age preferred to sit with their parents who were now coming, and teachers who had been sitting with the seniors felt they would rather go out half-way for class instruction. Nevertheless, the experience had been helpful during the early building up of the Family Service, and even though most children now left the service half-way through, the instruction given to adults was still kept pretty elementary, with visual aids, especially the overhead projector, which meant that newcomers did not feel out of their depth. Once a month we had Parade Service when juniors, seniors, and uniformed organizations remained in church for the whole service.

Those older than the seniors had their own Bible classes, meeting elsewhere and only coming into church in the morning at the monthly Parade Service. These arrangements were explained at some length to the Sunday School teachers so that it could be seen that, far from Family Service working in any opposition or competition with the Sunday School, in fact the two could work together in closest harmony, each depending upon the other.

Concerning the various age groupings and how we should cater for them, we would suggest the following breakdown:

Under three years: Crèche.

3–7 *years*: This is, as all parents know, a very *active* age, and it is probably better if children of this age do not come into the main worship except on very special occasions such as Mothering Sunday, Easter, Harvest and Christmas. Rather they should have their own meeting place for both worship and instruction. They will have the experience of arriving at church as a family, and could easily join their parents for refreshments afterwards. Admittedly, this means these children only come into the main service about four times a year, and this may not encourage their best behaviour on these rare occasions. However, there are usually lots of things to keep their attention, such as flowers to collect or fruit to deliver, etc.

8–11 *or* 12 *years:* This age group should come into the Family Service for the first half, but leave after that for instruction in classes.

12 *or* 13 *plus:* At this age the youngsters are beginning to flex their muscles of independence from the family, not in a spirit of rebellion necessarily, but in the natural processes of growing up and out. It would be a mistake to try to force young teenagers to come with their parents to Family Service every week. (Parade Service or special event are of course different.) It is far better to allow the teaching of this group to continue as a separate part of the church programme. Wherever possible, however, it ought to be at the same *time* as the Family Service, so that once again the family can begin and/or end together.

You will notice that we suggest 12 or 13 plus as the age of division. However, the educational structure in your neighbourhood may well determine your policy here. If secondary education is from 11 to 18, you might prefer to have your young team work start at 11 rather than wait till 13. On the other hand, if you have middle schools in your area, then obviously it will be easy to fit in with the local transition age of 12 or 13.

The bitter lesson that some members of the Sunday School staff may have to learn is that in spite of all the blessing and good that may have come in the past from a great movement, the Bible emphasizes that *parents* are primarily responsible for the spiritual upbringing of their own children, and the responsibility of the parish church is to *help* them do it, not take the job over entirely. The Family Service can be a real aid to parents in this direction.

My final statement I have been hesitant to put down. However, I believe this needs to be said, and I pray that the Holy Spirit will do His own work of convicting and convincing where the statement is true. Some childless Sunday School teachers, whether single or married, need to ask themselves before the Lord whether they are doing this this work among children for His sake *alone*, or partly because it provides them with a substitute family. For Family Service to succeed, Sunday School teachers have to be ready to make the sacrifice of handing back their pupils to the parents to whom they really belong.

2 Getting organized

Assuming that, despite possible misgivings by a small minority in the parish, it has been decided to go ahead with the institution of a Family Service, much preparation will be needed. This section is mainly concerned with initial practical arrangements, and the following sections with the service itself.

When do you start?

You should start when you are ready. In one sense this is a very misleading answer, for if you wait until you are ready you will never start. The Family Service is a developing experience, and in a lively church there will be a never-ending stream of ideas to improve the service, quite apart from the fact that if it is developing healthily there will be the constant need for ideas just to keep things ticking over—thinking about where to put a class that is getting too big, where to find new crèche helpers or class teachers, and so on. However, there are some matters that must have been arranged before the first service or you may never get started on a firm footing.

A number of people will make an effort to be present at the first service. It must go sufficiently well for them to be encouraged to come again, feeling that this is a band-wagon they must get on as early as possible. You must therefore allow yourself a reasonable amount of preparation time to be ready to that degree. Every Family Service promoter will, however, have his own idea of what degree of readiness there must be.

One should surely start at what seems to be the best time of the year. If I had my time over again, I would not change the time of year that my previous parish chose to commence the Family Service, so naturally I am biased about other possible times. We chose Harvest Thanksgiving Sunday, by tradition the first Sunday in October, for the following reasons (in approximately descending order of importance):

(a) It was an occasion when we naturally expected a lot of families to come to church in any case, so they could get a taste straight away of what had been planned for them. It was also an occasion when there were plenty of happy associations, with the church attractively decorated, the children bringing up fruit and flowers, and singing popular harvest hymns.

(b) It came at the end of the holiday season and not at a time when there was an unusual amount of sickness, so we expected to see faithful supporters there in strength.

(c) It was the start of a new school year.

(d) It was not too cold and wet, and wintry weather was not expected to set in for two or three months, so that the service had a chance to get established before numbers might temporarily drop for quite genuine reasons.

(e) It was the time of year when parishioners were used to receiving a printed leaflet through their letterbox about various regular autumn activities, and so were able to have their attention drawn to *An Important Notice about Service Changes*.

(f) Autumn and Christmas present several other occasions when infrequent churchgoers usually like to come, such as Remembrance Sunday, a Christmas Tree Service, Christmas Day Services, and the first Sunday of the new year.

(g) Families which go out for the day on Sundays have usually given this up for the winter by the beginning of October.

Adding all these factors together, I very much doubt if there is a better time of the year to start a Family Service than Harvest Thanksgiving Sunday.

Premises
It is no use embarking on a programme of Family Services and family evangelism without first taking a careful look at our church premises and ways in which we intend to foster the families who are joining us for worship.

Many are stuck with buildings which they would happily tear down and start again if it were possible, but with imagination even the worst premises can be improved. We need to think of ways in which we can make the new family feel at ease and able to participate fully in the whole service.

For example, it is vital to provide ample space. If it is a new experience for the family to step into church, the children will tend to cling to Mummy and Daddy. Nothing frightens a child more than to have to walk single file through a dark entrance, past a line of dark-suited men towering above a six-year-old, and then to creep down some long narrow aisle to a hard bench. No wonder some run screaming from the place! If you have pews to the back wall, rip some out (not forgetting the Faculty, of course!). If you get full you can always add stacking chairs. This extra space will also be useful for the coffee, about which we say more later on. Then have a bright notice board, an attractive bookstall with books for all ages, and service books and hymn books that are obviously cared for and which are handed personally to *each* member of the family. Nothing annoys a six-year-old more than to see his parents given books while he is neglected.

It has already been stressed that the main Family Service should take place in the parish church or at least in a consecrated building, but if Family Service is being combined with Sunday School there are other premises to consider. All places must be fairly close together. Age divisions will vary from place to place, but I would suggest that as a minimum, some room must be set aside firstly as a crèche for small children. This room must have moderately easy access for prams and a floor on which small children can play without danger. The vicar may have to be prepared to allow his vestry to be used in this way if accommodation is limited. A reasonable crèche age range would be up to three years old.

There will then be need for further accommodation for those between 3 and 7, who need a place by themselves where they will not be interrupted by the older children who come out from the main service half-way through. If premises are available it is desirable to split this age-group. Choir vestries could perhaps be called into service here, and the situation is simplified if the choir does not robe for the Family Service (see page 46).

Finally, yet another hall or large room will be necessary for the older children.

Free Church members may well find the accommodation question less of a bug-bear than Anglicans, owing to their policy of building schoolrooms adjoining the main worship room.

While I hold firmly to the view that withdrawal for instruction of the younger children is the best policy, I must add that I know of churches where there are thriving Family Services, in spite of the fact that lack of premises or lack of teachers has meant the children have to remain for the whole of the service. However, a crèche for under-3s is absolutely essential.

Some parishes may have sufficient hall space in the grounds of their church for the various age groups or, as the Family Service develops, may feel it necessary to build new halls if money allows. Should it be necessary to use halls any distance from the church, adequate provision must be made to see that any roads to be crossed between the church and the halls are manned at Family Service time.

In some areas proper provision may have to be made for the parking of cars. One church that has had a Family Service for over 30 years provides parking on popular Sundays for about 200 cars, and a policeman is on duty to guide them on to the busy main road after the service.

The premises having been decided on, some steps must be taken to see that they are provided with the bare essentials of equipment to cater for the appropriate age groups. Some parents of older children may be able to provide carrycots for the crèche, and some safe toys that might be kept there permanently. Once a few have been provided and the Family Service is well under way, the stock will almost automatically be replenished by those whose children grow out of the crèche. Chairs for the smaller children will be needed for the nursery and primary Sunday School: blackboards will also be required. But if you already have a Sunday School you will know what is needed, and indeed probably have these things already. One important rule should be that Family Service helpers are responsible for getting equipment out and putting it away, and that everything has its place. It is more than likely that the rooms, vestries and halls are going to be used again on the Sunday, and the Family Service will get a bad name if its staff are always leaving their equipment around. Like everything else in the church, things should be done 'decently and in order'.

Heat, light and sound

Whether or not you did science at school, this trilogy must be considered in connection with Family Service!

At whatever time of year you begin your Family Service, winter will come sooner or later, and so you must take every step to see your new congregation are not frozen away. Most people are reasonable enough to accept the fact that a large church building is a difficult place to *heat*. They will expect to wear their overcoats. But special care should be taken to make sure the heat is put on in time to enable the church to be warm at congregational level, that doors are not left open when people arrive, and the crèche and other rooms are kept warm too. If money is tight, it is probably psychologically better to heat the smaller and therefore less expensive rooms first, as parents will be prepared to make allowances if they are not too warm, but they will not forgive you if their young children are cold.

The *lighting* in many churches leaves much to be desired. Estimates for improvement can be very much higher than expected, and there will be many prior calls upon the parish purse before new lighting should be seriously considered. Indeed, when starting a Family Service there are other things more important than improved lighting, such as heat. However, one or two things can be done to make a big improvement to the lighting at comparatively small cost. For example, you could change the lights in the entrance to strip lighting, if that has not already been done, so that newcomers can find their way in easily without tripping, and so that you can see them really properly when you shake hands to say goodbye. Have good lights in the smaller rooms if the windows do not allow in plenty of light, as is so often the case in church buildings. Have lights over the hymn-board numbers, information table and bookstall. Finally, light up your visual aid board with a 100-watt spotlight which can be fitted into an adjustable shaded desk lamp.

If people, on entering the church, have their attention riveted by a large pool of light directed on to something colourful and attractive, meaningful or intriguing, this is going to help whet their appetite for the service, and they will overlook many shortcomings in the church. Remember in any case that in the average parish you are not catering for people with sensitive artistic tastes who want to admire the late-Victorian architecture, but those more used to stepping into the cinema, bingo hall or pub.

Sound is obviously important if we seriously believe in the concept of a 'ministry of the Word'. If God's Word cannot be heard clearly, we are wasting our time and that of others. This means that if a church is difficult acoustically something must be done about it. Professional advice needs to be sought, and some amplification installed; or perhaps such amplification as does exist needs boosting or modifying.

For professional advice I would particularly recommend Religious Recordings, 42 Gatesden Road, Fetcham, Surrey, KT22 9QR; telephone 037 23 73153 (Directors: Mr R. F. Chambers and Mrs R. V. Chambers). This firm has installed very proficient amplification in several churches including both my previous and present ones.

If such an outlay is not possible in the foreseeable future because of a tight budget, it is worth investigating the possibility of using a good tape recorder as an amplifier. This is by no means a crude alternative. For several weeks when our church amplifier was out of action, I adapted my tape recorder as an amplifier, and at least one elderly member of the congregation said she heard much better with it!

While on the subject of sound, there are one or two other suggestions worth considering. Obviously we should make sure we can be heard from the pulpit, lectern, and prayer reading desk. However, much that is done in a Family Service may be better conducted from the chancel steps, so we must make sure we have adequate provision for being heard there as well. In some churches it may be possible to do this by suspending a small inconspicuous microphone from the ceiling. But another method is to use a halter microphone. This need not be so luxurious as it sounds. In my own case I discovered quite by accident that my tape recorder microphone, which has a very long flex, could be plugged into the church amplifying system. It is wise to seek professional advice before taking such a step as this, but there may already be an electrical 'wizard' in a church who will freely give this expert advice.

A halter will cost under £1, and this can be worn round the neck and concealed under the surplice, so that most people in the congregation will be unaware of its existence, but very conscious of how remarkably well they can hear your voice even when you turn your head right round, perhaps to make an adjustment to a visual aid, while you are talking. A proper halter is so devised that the microphone can be attached or detached during the service. If you expect to be sharing the leading of Family Service with a curate or visiting speaker, it is wise to have a spare halter, as it is better put over the cassock and under the surplice before the service begins. Clergy need to be very humble about the audibility of their voices, for however loudly they may think they speak, the acoustics of some churches may well give rise to spots in the church where they cannot be heard at all.

Another suggestion worth bearing in mind is that a loudspeaker should be installed in the crèche so that the baby-sitters can have some share in the service, even if it may sometimes be drowned by other noises!

One final remark is to advise those using several visual aids, and perhaps a halter microphone, to mark the Order of Service sheet very carefully with directions of each main movement being made during the service. Otherwise at the critical moment when you need to switch on (say) the projector, you may find yourself attached by the halter to another part of the chancel!

Coffee

One of the main aims of Family Service is to bring in outsiders, and make them feel so welcome that they come again and again and eventually become 'one of us'. However, more often than not when they first come the only person they know is on the full-time staff. How do we get them to know other members of the congregation? The problem can be largely solved by serving coffee *in church*, so that when the newcomers make a dash for the door they are intercepted by someone offering them steaming coffee! Though some will have perfectly genuine reasons for refusing, but will none the less be impressed, a large number will be persuaded to stay. This gives the staff a chance to introduce them to other people, say of similar age and sex, perhaps living close to where they live. When I first introduced this into my previous parish I found it had an almost immediate effect on retaining reluctant worshippers, and I soon got to know them much better and also increased the size of my Confirmation Class.

It is important that these refreshments should be served in church, unless there is some vestibule which the congregation is obliged to go through in order to leave the building. As Rosamund Essex wrote recently in the *Church Times*:

'It is a sad truth about human nature that, if you invite the congregation to coffee and biscuits in the parish hall, half of the people get lost and never arrive, even though the hall may be but a few yards away. If they are asked to stay put in the church, and there are steaming urns at the ready as they troop out of their pews, they will be glad to stay—practically all of them. Of course you have your vergers to contend with, who have to sweep up the crumbs—how many baskets-full, they wonder.'

The practical details of arranging coffee will, of course, vary from place to place. In the church concerned we had the particular advantage of being able to unscrew our pews from the floor and move them away, so it was quite easy to create a coffee area at the back of the church. We had cups laid out before the service with instant coffee already in them and milk and sugar available. We borrowed the Youth Centre electric urn which we filled with water and plugged into an electric point at the back of the church. The urn was switched on before the sermon, and those responsible for making the coffee crept out to the back before the final hymn to pour it out. Screens, which could easily be removed during the final hymn, hid the coffee counter from the view of the people arriving for the service. A monthly rota of those responsible for the preparation of the coffee and the washing up afterwards can easily be made.

Alternatively disposable cups can be bought from a catering wholesalers, which solves the problem of washing up (and polystyrene cups solve the problem of scalding fingers). An insulated three-gallon urn with a tap, which has been filled with coffee before the service, gives coffee which is beautifully hot and refreshing an hour later and not too expensive an investment for the church. We go to places where we feel at home. If we feel uncomfortable we avoid them. Just notice how the public houses have changed their image in recent years: carpets, easy chairs, comfort, a home from home.

It is only fair to mention that the provision of coffee in church may not be immediately welcomed by some older and more traditional church members. They may, however, be strangely inconsistent, not hesitating to have tea brought round in church when they are helping with the cleaning on Friday or doing the flowers on Saturday, but finding it outrageous to serve coffee on Sunday in the very same place as part of our evangelism. Personally, I was so convinced of the rightness of serving coffee that I turned a pretty deaf ear to the complaints, pointing out that I ate and drank in church every Sunday at a fellowship meal on the instruction of none other than the Lord Jesus Himself. I also said that the point of serving the coffee was to create fellowship, which surely Jesus would approve. However, within a very short while of taking what appeared to some as unilateral action, the serving of coffee received almost unanimous approval because no one could deny that numbers were increasing, and there seemed to be a general reluctance by church members to leave the building after services, such was the warmth of the fellowship generated.

Recruiting

If the parish already has a Sunday School which is now combining with the Family Service, the more important helpers are already recruited. If there is no Sunday School, then personally I should not necessarily feel myself obliged to get all the helpers straight away, but to start the Family Service with all the children in church and select my helpers gradually and carefully as the Family Service develops. It is very much easier in parish work, which mostly depends on voluntary workers, to ask a suitable person to take on a job than to ask an unsuitable person to give it up.

If the hall space is very inadequate and not near the main church building, and there is no Sunday School either, then a regular Family Service with all ages together would seem to be the best course. However, every effort should be made from the very start to have a crèche not too far from the main service. Next to that it is best to provide for the 3- to 7-year-olds, as these ages can be a considerable disturbance to parents and other children, quite apart from irritating others that attend the service. After that I do not think I would provide for any others until I was reasonably sure I could introduce all age instruction for parents and children (see further in chapter 4).

Some capable person must be found to be in charge of the crèche. This person is not necessarily always on duty herself, but she is entirely responsible for selecting helpers and organizing a rota. Likewise the Family Service will need its own sidesmen, but again the organizing of this could be delegated, perhaps to one of the churchwardens. Personally I am not over-enthusiastic about having child sidesmen at Family Service, because it militates against the definition of the Family Service as mentioned in chapter 1. The children are not going to feel overlooked if they are not asked to do this sort of thing, whereas there is a very real danger of fathers coming to the service for the first time feeling they are being asked to take part in something slightly childish. If it is felt desirable for some local reason to keep the Sunday School collections separate from the adult collection, then that might be a very good reason for a child to bring up the children's collection bag, provided an adult brings up the adult collection. The various leaders who are responsible for finding further helpers must, of course, be given plenty of time to do so before the Family Service officially begins.

Advertising

It has been suggested earlier that a special leaflet should be distributed to every house or separate family unit in the parish. It might also be wise to design some simple little card that refers to the Family Service only, a copy of which can be given to every family with whom you have some contact, however slight.

CPAS has produced cards with its Family Worship motif printed on them, and a space for overprinting. Obvious contacts will be those on the Sunday School lists, Cradle Rolls, etc. If the parish has an assistant curate he might be specially freed to do some extensive visiting of homes where the Family Service idea might possibly be received with some enthusiasm. Alternatively, a team of Family Service visitors might be specially recruited to do a similar task fairly close to the start of the venture. The following is an example of the sort of printed card that can be distributed:

St John's Family Service
Every Sunday at 10 *am*

This weekly service is especially designed for parents and their children who find it difficult to attend the other church services. It is hoped that the time will suit everyone, so that there is still an opportunity to have a lie-in after a busy week's work, and yet still time to get the Sunday dinner, since the service finishes promptly at 10.45 am.

The service itself takes a simple form to suit all ages, with popular hymns and a short illustrated talk which it is hoped families will find bright, cheerful and helpful.

Children under 3 will be cared for by competent helpers in one of the halls adjoining the church.

It might also be worth while to get a competent amateur artist in the parish or, failing that, a professional, to prepare a design which can be made into a block for letterpress printing, or finished artwork for litho printing. This would be a fairly expensive outlay, but it is not necessarily extravagant when you realize it is going to be used time and time again.

The Family Service must also have a general build-up in the church magazine, more and more of the details being revealed in each edition. The issue for the month when you begin should have a real 'splash' about the Family Service, possibly even making some change in the magazine cover for that month only.

It is always a good idea to let the local press have a copy of your magazine each month in any case, but a tactful word in the editor's ear, requesting that he might refer to this service, may mean that reference will be made to your Family Service as a news item at no cost to yourself and without arousing any feeling from other churches that you are attempting to advertise in order to 'sheepsteal'.

A good poster should be put on the church notice-board and smaller window bills might be put in some local homes in the parish. Watch should also be kept to see how accurate the general notice-board announcing services is going to be once the great changeover comes. It is worth getting a proficient signwriter to change your board on the Monday immediately prior to the start of the Family Service. This may need plenty of advance notice. Finally, one should start giving out advance notice of the Family Service in church for several Sundays beforehand, and hand duplicated slips to Sunday School children for their parents. We need to make sure in our advertising that the children of light are just as wise in our generation as the children of this world!

Once the Family Service is under way it will be hoped that satisfied clients will pass the message around that the service is worth attending. Most children like wearing badges. CPAS has also produced badges with the Family Service motif, and these can be sold or given away to those attending. This could all be a further aid to advertising the service, especially in local schools.

3 The form of service

What sort of service should our Family Service most resemble, that of the Morning/Evening Prayer type, or Holy Communion?

To me there is simply no choice, for if the primary object of the service is evangelistic, that is, to bring outsiders to hear and receive the gospel, then Holy Communion is quite obviously inappropriate. This is not to say that there may not be a place for Family Communion in the general worship of the parish church. But this is not the type of Family Service with which we are primarily concerned in this book. I would, however, add in passing that I question the appropriateness of very young unconfirmed children attending Holy Communion. This is surely the occasion when the preacher should be speaking to the committed Christians in his parish. The sermon should contain what the Apostle Paul would describe as 'strong meat'. Yet for children this would inevitably be boring, and they would consequently be distracting to adult members of the congregation. If the preacher speaks so that the children will understand, the adults will not be adequately fed.

In some areas of the country few people are confirmed and increasing numbers unbaptized, so that to make a Family Service a service of Holy Communion would be absurd, for it would virtually discourage church attendance.

However, if All-age Instruction is being introduced (see chapter 4), then it might be appropriate for the final act of worship sometimes to be Holy Communion, even though some present may not yet be full believers. After all, the early Methodists are said to have regarded the Lord's Supper as a converting ordinance, meaning that it could have a strong evangelistic effect. It could also be right to have some children present (see chapter 5).

In areas where many people have been confirmed but rarely come to church, I would question how many of them are converted. I for one was brought up in a strata of society where to be confirmed at around the age of 14 was the accepted thing. All my friends were.

I should have been very much the odd boy out if I had not been. So I went through the classes, made all the right noises to the chaplain, and was duly presented to the bishop and confirmed. But it was not till eight years later that I first began to grasp what the Christian gospel was really about, and my experience is, of course, by no means unique.

There will be more in chapter 7 about the problem of indiscriminate baptism, but for some parishes the more serious problem may be that of indiscriminate confirmation. If a parish consists of many unconverted, non-churchgoing parents, who happen for one reason or another to have been confirmed, it surely cannot really be argued that a Family Service based on Holy Communion should be provided for them. I believe it is the simple straightforward gospel, presented in a simplified Morning Prayer type of service, that will be most appropriate to their need.

This simplicity is no handicap as far as the adults are concerned. For many years I was associated with the beach mission work of the Children's Special Service Mission (now officially named the Scripture Union), and I can think of quite a number of parents from very respectable backgrounds, confirmed of course (it would a social stigma to be otherwise), who, after hearing a simple talk on the beach, designed primarily for their young children, have confided in me that for the first time they have come to put their trust in Jesus Christ as their Saviour. At least one such person is now an ordained minister of the Church of England.

So our service is to be a simplified form of Morning Prayer. In 1966 Michael Cole, then a vicar in Sheffield and later at Holy Trinity, Platt, Manchester, wrote to me suggesting that an attempt ought to be made to draw up some sort of 'national' order of service for family worship. Likeminded people joined us, and we set up regional committees of which the chairmen were to be on a central coordinating committee. By means of the church press we discovered information about some 40 existing Family Services, and examples of the liturgy used, of which, incidentally, only three were based on Holy Communion. Some replies came from clergy responsible for English-speaking congregations overseas, for example in South Africa and the Channel Isles. In the course of preparation of *An Order of Family Service* (Appendix A) some 250 clergy were consulted for their advice, and some 35 congregations used the interim service for six months and submitted their observations.

Of course, there are some special occasions in the year where variations will need to be made, and when the service will probably be longer.

In many churches on such occasions as Mothering Sunday, Harvest or Christmas, children come up to the chancel to give or receive something. Toys or harvest gifts are best received during an opening hymn; things like flowers on Mothering Sunday are best given out at the end. It is usually wise to have an extra hymn provisionally planned if these operations are likely to last some time.

On Remembrance Sunday, special provision must be made for the two minutes' silence, which should come at 11.00 am. For example, if the Family Service begins at 10.00 am allow the service to continue until 11.04.

Calculate as accurately as possible when the sermon must end, and make sure to have several extra illustrations in the sermon that can be used as time-fillers if required.

Family Worship

The first edition of *Family Worship* was published in 1971 and contained the Family Service mentioned above (slightly amended), some original prayers, psalms from the Old and New Testaments, and some hymns and choruses mostly from Scripture Union, Youth Praise and what was later to be Psalm Praise. A revised edition was published in 1975 which also included services for Mothering Sunday and Harvest and a Christmas Gift Service, and Series 2 Baptism.

Family Worship has some numbered pages at the back which are otherwise blank; parishes can stick their own material here. The book can also be useful as a supplementary hymn book at other services.

4 Hymns and things

Some years ago a parishioner admitted to me that she had felt convicted before the Lord concerning the use of her tongue long before I had announced my sermon text from James 3. Of course, this was the Holy Spirit's work, but He had been enabled to use the hymns and two lessons to cause this lady's conviction, because they had all been chosen on the theme of the use and misuse of the tongue.

It has always been my policy in the Family Service to have a theme for each week and to design every variable part to fit into it. Conversation with regular worshippers has shown me that this policy is appreciated and aids attention. Christopher Robin was neither the first nor the only person to have trouble with wandering thoughts during his prayers. If we can help our Family Service worshippers in this sort of way, then we should.

Hymns

Hymns should be sung from the regular church hymn book unless the parish can afford some other book that would not be too obviously childish for adults to use. *Family Worship*, mentioned above, can be used as an alternative hymn book sometimes.

We need to keep the service short in any case, so it is best to avoid hymns that are too long, perhaps omitting verses if necessary. In any case a lengthy hymn can easily bore young children. Another device in overcoming the problem of long hymns is to divide them, singing the first part before the sermon and remaining verses afterwards, telling the congregation to keep their books open during the sermon. It is occasionally useful to quote a verse of that closing hymn at the end of the talk before the rest of the hymn is sung, as a means of pressing home the message of the Family Service for that day.

It is wise to make sure that the opening hymn is well known, and that the majority of the tunes are known. If a new tune is introduced, it is a good idea to get the organist to extemporize on the tune as a voluntary, so that the congregation will at least feel it is familiar. There is much to be said for being honest about a new tune—we can tell the congregation we feel sure it will be popular when heard a few times, and get it played through before being sung for the first time.

Choir

In some parishes, especially the more residential ones, it may be easy either to provide a special choir for the Family Service or to use the existing one. The formation of a special Family Service choir of children may be an incentive for some families to start coming. In other areas, however, provision of a choir may be quite out of the question, and to use the existing one may produce further problems because Sunday School teachers may be choir members as well. In this situation it seems better to dispense with a robed choir. This is not necessarily all loss, because if there are some choir members to form part of the congregation they may greatly boost the singing from there. If there is a choir it may be better to place it somewhere in front of the reading desk so that members can see any visual aid being used, as well as hear better.

Psalms and canticles

As an Anglican I believe it is right that Psalms and canticles should form part of the Family Service, otherwise Family Service worshippers will not become familiar with them should they later attend Morning or Evening Prayer. However, I would strongly question whether these should be chanted, because most newcomers find chants very strange and impossible to sing. *Family Worship* provides some metrical Psalms and canticles, and *Psalm Praise* has plenty more. If tradition demands that some chanted Psalms or canticles must be used, *Family Worship* provides a selection of shorter ones, together with some passages from the New Testament which can be sung to chants and which are especially suitable at the major festivals. The *Te Deum* and *Benedicite* are probably best not sung in full, although part could be used. especially if there is a choir. If there is no choir, it may be better to say them; though on a Sunday when an especially good congregation is expected, well-known Psalms like numbers 23, 46, 67, 100, 121 or 150 might be sung quite safely.

Choruses

There seems to be no objection to the use of choruses in Family Services, but something needs to be said about the way they are used. First, the value of singing through a number before the service begins, and having a session during the service, seems doubtful. We are almost encouraging the congregation to take the Lord's name in vain through superficiality. A chorus is really only a short, simple spiritual song. One or two them of should be selected carefully to fit in with the theme of the service.

Secondly, they probably ought not to be chosen by the children during the service, because this leads to two difficulties: either certain choruses are sung every week, or else the congregation has to try to sing a chorus that no one knows, often not even the person leading the service! Further, there is always the problem that some child is going to be disappointed, and if time is a factor it is very difficult to assess how long this part of the service is going to take. Some churches do allow children to choose a chorus if their birthday falls in the same week as the service, but this practice usually militates against the general theme policy.

If choice by the congregation is desired, it seems best that worshippers should be encouraged to let the leader of Family Service know not only choruses but even hymns they like, and these can be fitted into services when they are suitable. The uncertainty of when their hymn is going to be sung might help regular attendance by those who have made the requests! Occasionally a chorus should especially be included for the youngest children, but when this is the case it should be clearly stated, in order that older children and adults are not made to feel a little awkward at singing what is obviously rather juvenile. Choruses are better accompanied on the piano or guitar, as also are some hymns. It is important that the piano is sited fairly close to the organ to enable the organist to move easily from one to the other. Piano and organ together can also be very effective if the musical talent is available. If there is a spare microphone, this might be placed near the piano.

With choruses as with hymns, it is important not to use a book which is too childish for adult use. *Family Worship* also includes a reasonable range of choruses, including some with well-known actions, especially suitable for younger children.

Music
It can be a real aid to worship if some pleasant music can be played on the organ or piano before and after the service, and during the collection, whatever form this takes. It need not be an organ version of the latest pop tune, but in choosing suitable music the organist should consider the degree of musical appreciation of the congregation, which will obviously vary from area to area.

Lessons
Whether one or two lessons are included, they should be well read, and of course properly amplified (see page 37). For this reason it is probably best not to use a child; he or she would have to be a quite exceptional reader, and even then the lesson should be heard in advance. Likewise, *any* layman should not be chosen but should be heard privately before the service. Whoever does the reading, there should be plenty of time for preparation. We should also choose our readers with imagination. A mother with a good reading voice might be asked to read the lesson on Mothering Sunday, for example.

The version of the Bible used should be the one that most people will have, which is probably in these days the RSV, though NEB and TEV are becoming increasingly popular. If a modern translation is selected, it should be made clear that this will be the version used week by week, and new copies should be available on the church bookstall to purchase. Some churches may be able to afford to provide Bibles in the appropriate version for the pews. Once a version has been selected, it should be adhered to; children find it very confusing if they cannot follow the lesson through even though they know they have found the right place. The lesson should not be too long, normally between 12 and 15 verses, and usually of the story variety, which will probably mean from the Gospels, Acts, or the historical parts of the Old Testament.

The competition

An innovation that came fairly early into our Family Service was the 'criss-cross quiz'. This is a competition between boys and girls based on the lesson that has just been read, combined with a game of noughts and crosses (of course the children may also be divided into teams or in other ways). It is played as follows:

The boys are asked a question; if one of them answers correctly, a large 'B' is placed on a flannelgraph or teazlegraph board in a square of their choosing (as in the game of noughts and crosses). The girls are then given a question, and if one of them answers correctly a 'G' is placed in a square of their choosing. There are various special rules that we have found necessary, such as no child being allowed to answer two questions consecutively.

Although we have been doing this for several years now, the interest never seems to flag, and adults often express to me how they enjoy this part of the service. It does create a very informal and friendly atmosphere between the congregation and those conducting the service. Adults may not have to answer the questions verbally, but they are challenged to see whether they can answer them in the privacy of their own minds. We find that the children are getting very good both at answering the questions and at noughts and crosses!

A visiting preacher once expressed to me his astonishment at the silence during the reading of the lesson. He was completely mystified, until the criss-cross quiz started, which explained all. Before the service we place the lesson text (the name of the book of the Bible and the chapter number) on the board, deliberately omitting the verse numbers to be read. This is to encourage the children to look up the passage and read the chapter, thereby giving them something profitable to do before the service starts.

There are of course many other kinds of competitions which can be used in the same way.

Prayers

There should be some set prayers in a Family Service, some of which

could be said together. Care should be taken not to rush them, especially the Lord's Prayer and the General Confession. Even if there is a
section of the service where extra prayers can be included, it is best
not to have too many. A short extempore prayer may sometimes be
helpful, or a short and simple litany. Collects in modern English from
Guy Daniel's *The Enemy is Boredom*,[1] from Susan William's *Lord of
our World*[2] and those produced by Akehurst and Bishop to accompany
the new lectionary[3] are specially recommended. *Family Worship* also
has quite a variety of suitable prayers. We need to be careful that the
time of prayer does not become what W. E. G. Allan calls 'shuffling
boredom'.[4]

It may be possible to get a family to be responsible for the prayer
section, in which case the following directions are to be recommended:

Begin with the Family Prayer (the Lord's Prayer)
Prepare three or four other prayers (there are plenty of suggestions in
Family Worship)
End with the 'Prayer for families and homes' in *Family Worship*.
Please stand *close* to the microphone so that everybody's voice is
picked up.

If a child is to read a prayer, please make sure that his voice comes
across the microphone, either by lifting him up or lowering the neck
of the microphone.

Notices
In my previous church we had the notices first to avoid disrupting the
theme of the service. The disadvantage of this is that some people
usually miss them, whether by design or accident! In any case, notices
should be as short as possible. Really important notices, especially if
they affect the children, are best duplicated and given out to be taken
home. Some churches duplicate the notices every week.

Collection
A number of churches nowadays have dispensed with taking a collection during the services, relying instead on a plate or box at the
entrance to the church. This practice has much to commend it in any
case, but especially at the Family Service, because it saves time during

[1] Guy Daniel, *The Enemy is Boredom* (Darton, Longman and Todd, 1964).
[2] Susan Williams, *Lord of our World* (Falcon, 1973).
[3] *Collects with the new lectionary* (Grove Books, Bramcote, Notts.).
[4] W. E. G. Allan, *Notes on a Sunday Family Service* (SPCK, 1965).

the service and avoids money being dropped or played with by children before the collection is made. It also facilitates a separate 'Sunday School' collection (see page 41).

Finally
Everything needs to be done to encourage peace of mind in parents and children before the service starts. New families need to be welcomed, the younger children introduced to the person they will meet when they go elsewhere for their own instruction. And with regard to that point in the service, it does seem better to have a purposeful disturbance rather than somewhat hypocritical hymn or chorus-singing designed to be the right length to 'get the children out'.

Each step of the service needs to be announced every week. Remember children do not find page numbers or hymn numbers as quickly as adults. Mention about joining in, saying 'Amen', what posture to adopt and so on. This can all be done quite naturally and helps new families to feel at home and at one with what is happening—they might even come again.

3 Speaking at a Family Service

One of the direct results of the first edition of *Reaching the Families* was a request for a volume of talks suitable for use in Family Services. This led to the publication in 1973 of *Teaching the Families*.[1] There seems to be little point in repeating here what has already been written there. I propose therefore to make some general observations about the art of speaking at Family Services, and then attempt to analyse in some detail how three talks of mine came into existence. John Tigwell will add some thoughts on speaking at Family Services from the layman's point of view.

1 Children and adults together

As explained earlier, there will be times when it is better for the family to divide up for the instruction period. However, there will be occasions when children of (say) 8 years old and upwards (very occasionally younger) and their parents are all together in church for the Family Service. From some parishes this could be every Sunday, for others perhaps monthly. This need not be a serious disadvantage because both often require the same degree of simplicity. Dr Martyn Lloyd-Jones[2] tells of a letter from a 12-year-old girl written on behalf of herself and her brother which he especially treasures. 'You are the only preacher we can understand', she stated. Dr Lloyd-Jones later goes on to explain that the source of his own policy is none other than the great German Reformer Martin Luther.

'"A preacher", says Luther, "should have the skill to teach the unlearned simply, roundly and plainly; for teaching is of more importance than exhorting." Then he adds, "When I preach I regard neither doctors nor magistrates, of whom I have above forty in the congregation. I have all my eyes on the servant maids and the children. And if the learned men are not well pleased with what they hear, well, the door is open." That, surely, is the right attitude. Some "doctors and magistrates" perhaps may feel like that, that not sufficient attention is being paid to them by the preacher in the pulpit. But the wise preacher keeps his eye on the servant maids and the children. If this great and learned man feels that he does not get anything he is condemning himself. He is condemning himself in the sense that he is not spiritually minded, that he is not able to receive spiritual truth. He is so "puffed up" and blown up with his head knowledge that he

[1] *Teaching the Families*, ed. Michael Botting (Falcon, 1973).
[2] *Preaching and Preachers* (Hodder and Stoughton, 1971), page 128.

has forgotten that he has a heart and soul. He condemns himself, and if he walks out, well, he is the loser. I am assuming, of course, that the preacher is really preaching the Word of God!'

However, in attempting to make Family Worship simple we must not go to the other extreme and reduce everything to the lowest common denominator. 'It is part of experience to be involved sometimes in situations which we cannot fully understand. Without this there would be no real challenge or "stretch" in the learning processes.

The lack of response of the young is seen when the whole situation, for the whole time, is beyond their comprehension.' Besides, 'adult members need themselves to be able to participate positively; not as spectators of some children's activity and not patronizingly taking an interest in what is happening. Their involvement in the worship at every stage, as mature Christians, becomes an essential part of the "atmosphere", the mysterious element at the heart of all worship which makes the exercise of Christian worship unique. Children may not understand everything that happens, but they are very sensitive to "atmosphere". A sense of being part of this, caught up in it; an awareness of something bigger than themselves which is important for their elders but in which they are able to share; this is part of their Christian education and part of their experience of belonging to a Christian community.'[1]

Certain simple steps can be taken to make sure both adults and children feel they are part of the congregation. When illustrations are given both groups should be considered: for example, in a talk on prayer we might be making the point that we can pray at any time and in any place, and mention can be made of offering up a prayer in school, and also praying at work or in the kitchen. In a longer illustration, a story involving adults can be just as intelligible to children.

Another device that can sometimes be used is that of speaking at different speeds, so that adults can take the point you are making quickly whereas children will miss it. Sometimes slightly humorous but kindly remarks can be made at the expense of the children or adults, which will help to maintain a reasonably informal atmosphere in the service, as well as binding the two age groups in the congregation together. Care should always be taken to ensure that the preacher's voice never sounds in any sense patronizing.

[1] From *Together in Church*, published by the Methodist Youth Department, page 7.

2 Visual aids

From the most cursory glance at *Teaching the Families* it will be evident that visual aids are an important feature of the Family Service talk. Some leaders may question this, feeling that the visual is overdone. Those who read this book will be those who are used to reading, and probably their chief complaint is that they do not get enough time for it; but a large section of the community, including the very people we want to attend Family Service, have a strong aversion to the printed page and prefer a much more direct, visual and sensory channel of communication. Richard Hoggart makes this clear in *The Uses of Literacy*[1], and John Benington in *Culture, Class and Christian Belief* makes the same point:[2]

'The challenge to Christianity is not to try and "educate" working-class people to a higher level of mental development which would enable them to grasp religious concepts; nor (and this is a more common approach) to try and translate the concepts into more intelligible "modern" terms: but much rather to try and "enter in" to the quite different mode of perception among the working-class, and to try and see what the Christian gospel looks like, and feels like, from this stance. One must be prepared to stand aside from the concepts and doctrines which have defined Christianity for oneself, and, beginning with the concrete facts of everyday experience, wait to discover those points at which Christian concepts in fact "ring true" to the situation. . . .

'Christ's own use of metaphor and parable reminds one first of McLuhan's[3] ideas about global sensation and all-at-once perception, and then of the working-class preference for concrete graphic description rather than abstract conceptual analysis. His parables often referred to familiar day-to-day situations (sowing, vineyards, salt, lamps, weddings and so on) and these were used as metaphors, as the occasion for a disclosure about God, or about Christ Himself.'

However, like money and sex, visual aids can be good servants but bad masters. I would stress therefore that we should first seek to ascertain the Lord's message, and then decide whether a visual aid might be used to *aid* the presentation of that message. Some so-called aids can be a positive hindrance to both speaker and audience,

[1] Chatto and Windus 1957.
[2] Scripture Union (1973) pages 70–71.
[3] For an introduction to the new world of Marshall McLuhan, begin by reading *McLuhan Hot and Cool*, ed. G. E. Stearn (Penguin).

in that only the aid is remembered and the message is forgotten. However, it would be hypocritical not to admit that sometimes an idea for a visual aid has provoked me to see a message from the Lord, and this was the method of men like Jeremiah and Amos, who saw a boiling pot, a plumbline or a basket of rotting summer fruit, and this led them to proclaim, 'Thus says the Lord . . .' But generally speaking it is a bad principle to select the aid and then find a message to fit it!

Story-telling
There is of course no rule that a visual aid must always be used in a Family Service. Often a biblical or other story, vividly told, is by far the most effective way of capturing the imagination and holding the attention. David Lewis devotes a chapter to this in *Teaching the Families* (pages 19–24).

However, we need also to remember that in using visual aids we are in the perfect company of the master teacher of all, Jesus Himself. He would point to the lilies of the field, the sower, the shepherd and his flock, the fig-tree, the harvest-time, the sunset and a host of other things, using them as visual aids. Finally He took bread and wine to illustrate the meaning of His passion.

It also needs to be remembered that story-telling was in His day one of the main ways in which people entertained one another. Jesus used this to 'get across' divine truth. A very little reflection will show that much of His teaching was by means of stories, and they were not religious ones either. Religion very rarely came into them, and when it did it was usually at a discount—for example, the priest and the Levite from the Good Samaritan, or the Pharisee and the publican who went to pray. Today's medium of entertainment is still largely by story-telling, but with the help of television or the cinema, that is, visual aid. Surely Jesus would have used visual methods nowadays to get across divine truth.

No notes
Talks should normally be given from the chancel steps rather than in the pulpit (provided you can be seen), and if you are using a visual aid you will need to keep your hands as free as possible. This means that sermon notes will have to be almost, if not entirely, abandoned. This may take a little time, but it is a very great gain. Provided you have prepared thoroughly beforehand, you can surely rely wholly on the Holy Spirit to bring to your remembrance all that you have to say.

Besides, if you are using a visual aid that really does fit the talk, it should be an aid to memory in itself.

Delegation
If you find it a problem to produce visual aids of an adequate quality, there is such a thing as delegation. There may well be talent in the most surprising quarters just waiting to be used. The Rev. Rex Bird, Rector of Lavenham (writing in the quarterly broadsheet ACE) says, 'I have been able to use visual aids extensively with the help of local artists—ranging from a member of the Royal Academy to a retired cartoonist of the *Daily Sketch*.' He goes on; 'Everything from a full-size dinghy to a twelve-foot snake (stuffed) has been used to illustrate the talk.' We must pray that God the Holy Spirit will bring to our notice those to whom He has given these gifts.

Cost of equipment
For too long the church has been associated with the second-rate, with the serious consequence that the Christian message has instinctively been given a similar coding. People almost expect the church projector to fail. We should therefore take every reasonable precaution to make sure our audio-visual aids are efficient, and this may mean not using the cheapest equipment.

How do we afford these items? I have reasoned this way: God expects me to be a good steward of the money He has committed to me. He expects me to set aside at least a tenth especially for His work. It is also my responsibility before Him how that tenth is allocated. I therefore allocate part of it, in fact about a tenth, for such expenses. The result is that I possess some good equipment available for the church to use, such as a slide and filmstrip projector, tape recorder, screen, teazlegraph, etc., at no cost to the PCC. But because these are mine and not just the parish's, I am inclined to keep them in good order. Expenses can also be kept down by making use of the grants for equipment for church purposes and by purchasing some things in bulk. By the time I left my first living the PCC had come to see the value of such equipment, and bought quite a lot of it from me, which was helpful as my next parish was enlightened enough to possess most of it already.

3 Preparation
It needs to be stressed that the Family Service is not a subsidiary

service but very much a service in its own right, and the talk may well need *much more* preparation than other sermons. It is well worth spending time and trouble over. In other spheres such as music and advertising, simplicity is often achieved after much toil and sweat, though the final production may seem so obvious and clear. Dr Martyn Lloyd-Jones in his most inspiring and helpful, as well as entertaining, book *Preaching and Preachers*[1] speaks of struggling to get the matter of a sermon into the right divisions.

I once heard the late R. Hudson Pope, revered children's evangelist on the staff of the CSSM (now Scripture Union) admit that in his early years as a Christian worker he had heard Josiah Spiers (founder of the CSSM) give a children's address. Mr Pope went straight home and tore up the notes of every children's talk he had ever given, and thus opened a new era of children's talks for him and many thousands of people of all ages who have been blessed by his ministry.

Those who say that Family Service talks are just not their metier have two courses open to them: either not to attempt to start a Family Service, with the possible loss to the work of evangelism that might result; or to be prepared to put their shoulder to the wheel and train themselves. Surely those who have been ordained to preach the Gospel should be prepared to take serious trouble to learn new arts.

Syllabus

In Appendix B there is a three-year syllabus for use at Family Services. It includes suggested subjects for every Sunday for three years, together with a talk for Good Friday and Christmas Day. It was prepared on the assumption that it would be used from the first Sunday in September to the last Sunday in August.

Defining your aims

When you have selected your text, subject or story, it must be thoroughly examined with all the normal aids used in sermon preparation, such as other versions of the text, including Greek or Hebrew if known, and commentaries, so that the main teaching is grasped by you personally. It is a good practice to write down in a few words what is to be one's aim in the talk and what Christian doctrine one is really attempting to impart. If this is difficult, then it probably means that you yourself are not clear on this, and that therefore your audience will certainly not be clear either. It is better to plan to make one point

[1] Hodder and Stoughton, 1971 (page 210).

that will be remembered than several that will be forgotten. It is also important not to feel that every part of a story or parable has to be explained. You should make sure you really do teach what the passage says and avoid attempting to turn every talk into a so-called 'gospel' address. Likewise, one should obviously not attempt to declare the 'whole counsel of God' in every talk.

Beginnings and endings

These are obviously important moments in the talk and need special care in preparation. The former must grasp and keep the attention of the congregation when it is at its best; the latter is important because the last thing said could well be the one point remembered.

Deciding the method of approach

When Nicodemus sought out Jesus one night his opening remarks were significant: 'We know that you are a teacher come from God'. We can go further than Nicodemus; we know that Jesus is *the* teacher come from God, so obviously we should be able to learn from Him different methods of approach in teaching divine truth.

(i)   The question and answer method

Illustrations of this are legion, for example Matthew 22.41–46:

'Now while the Pharisees were gathered together, Jesus asked them a question, saying, "What do you think of the Christ? Whose son is he?" They said to him, "The son of David." He said to them, "How is it then that David, inspired by the Spirit, calls him Lord, saying,

'The Lord said to my Lord,
Sit at my right hand,
till I put thy enemies under thy feet'?

If David thus calls him Lord, how is he his son?" And no one was able to answer him a word, nor from that day did any one dare to ask him any more questions.'

The main points to watch about this method are to know where you are going and ask your questions carefully, having worked each one out beforehand. We should not readily answer our own questions, but rephrase them or give hints until the right answer is given. If we frequently find our questions are too difficult, the fault lies with us, and we should make a serious attempt to be simpler. A balance must be struck between appealing to the children's natural curiosity about the answer and wearying them so that they 'couldn't care less'.

Care must be taken to accept answers from different children and to encourage the more timid children by accepting the answers to easier questions from them. Always give credit for an attempted answer even if wide of the mark. A particularly interesting way in which Jesus used the question and answer method in preaching, was in asking for a verdict from His hearers. For example, in the parable of the Good Samaritan, He asks:

' "Which of these three, do you think, proved neighbour to the man who fell among the robbers?" He (the lawyer) said, "The one who showed mercy on him". And Jesus said to him, "Go and do likewise".' (Luke 10.36–37)

(ii) Direct story-telling

Jesus did this mostly with His parables, and evidently to such effect that He had His audience entirely captivated, so much so that they chimed in (see Luke 19.25, part of the parable of the pounds).

This method can be used very well with Old Testament stories and incidents in the Gospels and the Acts. Plenty of imagination should be applied, including perhaps some anachronisms to give the stories a modern up-to-date twist; for example in the story of Naaman, the leper, who mistakenly goes to the King of Israel for healing, you might suggest that Elisha got 'on the blower' to the King to tell him to send Naaman down to him![1]

Even a bit of dramatic action can be effective, perhaps by pointing at an imaginary sower sowing seed, or acting the part of Bartimaeus calling for Jesus.

In telling any historical story we can often add greatly to the interest and understanding of the story if there is a good map, either printed or carefully drawn on a blackboard or overhead projector, and referred to regularly. In this type of talk the important thing is for the speaker to have a thorough grasp of the story himself, and to practise it on his own several times, preferably in the place where the talk will actually be given. Doing this may sometimes suggest improvements. The remarks earlier in the chapter about doing without notes are especially applicable in this case.

It is worth noticing also that in several of Jesus' stories he used repetition to aid memory, eg in the parables of the pounds, the talents, and the lost sheep, silver and son (see Luke 19, Matthew 25, Luke 15). Further details may be found in Teaching the Families, pages 19–24.

[1] David Kossoff's books of Bible stories are a perfect example of this imaginative, anachronistic story-telling.

(iii)   Teaching based especially on a visual aid
As was said earlier, Jesus often used visual aids, and just as some of His talks revolved entirely round one (a sower, or a child, for example) so can some of ours. But care must be taken that the points are not forced and that there is a clear biblical warrant for the points being made.

Under this heading we might include the type of talk which uses a number of well-chosen words or pictures to summarize the talk as it is given. A talk on Bartimaeus, for example, can be simply illustrated by his name itself, and then 'many hindered', 'some helped' and 'one healed'. With this approach the lessons can often be applied in stages as you proceed, instead of all the points coming at the end when attention may have flagged. The visual aids can be put on cards which rest on carefully placed pins on a blackboard, or put on a flannelgraph board, teazlegraph or overhead projector; or alternatively they can be chalked on a blackboard beforehand and covered with black card (held in position by pins or Sellotape) which is removed at the appropriate moments. Speed is essential whichever method is used.

(iv)   The use of filmstrips and films
However good may be one's powers of description, a good filmstrip will give an audience a much better picture of the background and customs of biblical characters and incidents. It is obviously quite impossible to black out most churches for a filmstrip in the middle of the morning. However, from about September to April filmstrips or coloured slides can be used effectively by means of a daylight screen. Full details about the construction of this, together with other information about the use of films and filmstrips in Family Services, can be found in *Teaching the Families* pages 40–46.

Once the screen has been constructed and erected, you need to place behind it a 1,000 watt (or equivalent) projector fitted with a filmstrip (or slide) carrier. The filmstrip itself must not only be put into the carrier upside down, but also back to front! When the projector is switched on and focused, a brilliant picture will be seen by members of the congregation.

It is also possible to use the daylight screen for projecting a film, although this is slightly more complicated because on normal makes of cineprojector you cannot thread the film through back to front. The way to overcome this difficulty is to project the film through a good quality mirror placed at an angle of 45° to both projector and screen, as illustrated.

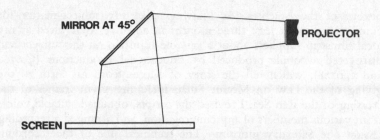

A further advantage of back projection is that all the wires are out of the way of the congregation, and no one can stand in the light to cause shadows on the screen. The screen can also be used very effectively for evening films or soundstrips.

I would suggest that this kind of audio-visual aid should only tell the story, and any introductory remarks or concluding application should be given 'live'. The use of a film or filmstrip does not absolve the minister from adequate preparation.

(v) Other methods
Teaching the Families gives information about the use of the overhead projector, congregational participation, drama and the use of puppetry, together with outline talks illustrating the use of these means of presenting Christian truth in the Family Service.

Writing your talk
When one has decided one's text, aim, and method of approach, the whole talk should be outlined, and in the early years written out word for word. This will greatly assist the speaker to make sure that each part of the talk follows in a logical sequence, and that every illustration has been thought through in advance.

The importance of beginnings and endings has already been mentioned, but it is useful to make a definite point about two-thirds of the way through, when interest might well be flagging. A good illustration or the production of a visual aid at that moment may help bring the talk to a successful end.

4   The construction of three Family Service talks

(a) The Crossing of the Red Sea
This is the sort of talk that might be given in a weekly series on the

history of the Israelites. As I always plan my subject-matter for Family Services at least three months in advance, I enquired at my local filmstrip suppliers about a suitable filmstrip on this subject and discovered a couple produced by Educational Productions (C.6160 and C.6128), which tell the story of Moses from his birth to the giving of the Law on Mount Sinai, including vivid frames of the crossing of the Red Sea. I revised the scripts, obtained suitable voices from various members of my congregation, and arranged a recording session one Saturday morning. The technical side of the recording was provided by another member of the congregation who happens to work on the technical side of the BBC. The resulting soundstrip would provide the basic story of part the talk.

Next, I realized that the congregation also needed to see exactly what the historical and geographical situation was when Pharaoh and his 600 chariot force descended on the Israelites. Here I brought the overhead projector into play, drawing the map opposite in various colours.

Now the basic biblical material was available in audible and visual form. What was the message of the Old Testament story for people of the 1970s? I jotted down the following facts:

The Israelites needed saving.
It was a matter of life or death, or worse slavery.
Unless God intervened, there was no way out of their predicament, but that is exactly what God did—He intervened. (A quote from the 1662 Baptism Service came to mind: 'And also didst safely lead the Children of Israel, Thy people, through the Red Sea.')
The Israelites had to make a choice.

Here was a straightforward 'Gospel' message which finally took the following shape:

Have you ever found yourself in a corner—just not knowing which way to turn? The Israelites, whom we were thinking about last week, got into that situation after leaving Egypt.

(I showed the filmstrip. Immediately after the end of the filmstrip, I switched on the overhead projector which had also been erected alongside the filmstrip projector behind the daylight screen. I pointed out the route which the Israelites would probably have taken to reach the Red Sea from Egypt.)

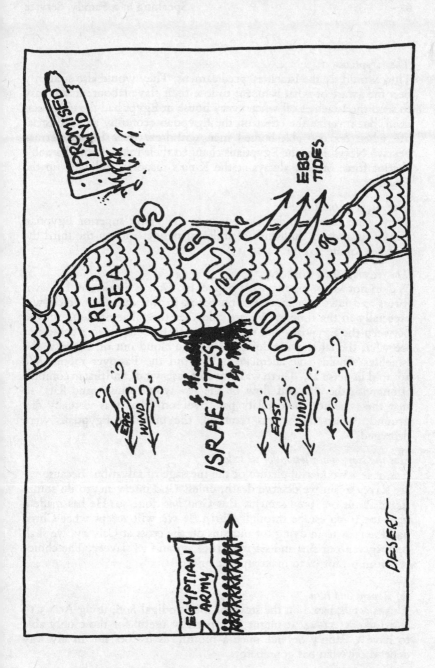

The Egyptians
They would see the Israelites' predicament. They would also suddenly become aware of what it meant to lose their slave labour: it was easy to send the Israelites off when every house in Egypt had the eldest son dead, but imagine the effect on the Egyptian economy and industrial life when 600,000 able-bodied men withdrew their labour permanently! No wonder the Egyptians changed their minds! So, Pharaoh's chariot force of 600, always at the King's disposal, followed up the Israelites.

The plight of the Israelites
They were in a triangle. On one side the vastly superior Egyptian army; on another thousands of miles of desert; and on the third the Red Sea (quote Exodus 14.13–15).

The crossing of the Red Sea
We do not know exactly what happened. God as a rule uses His own forces and laws to achieve His purposes. In this case the miracle was especially in the timing. We are told that the pillar of cloud moved between the Egyptians and the Israelites so that the former could not see what the latter were doing. With the cloud out of the way, the Israelites would have adequate light from the Passover moon. We are told in verse 21, 'There was a strong east wind', and that in combination with the ebb and flow of the sea would cause mud flats, so that the Israelites could easily pass over on what was virtually dry ground. When the waters returned, the pursuing Egyptians were drowned.

Has the story got a lesson for us today?
Yes, it is a wonderful picture of the message of salvation. Because we are slaves to sin we deserve death, unless God intervenes to do something about our predicament. But God *has* done so. He has made a way for us to escape through Christ. If we will accept what Christ has done for us in dying for our sins on the cross at Calvary, we shall be forgiven our sins and set free from sin and its slavery. The choice is before us, for us to make up our minds.

(b) Repent and turn
This is a talk based on the story of the Prodigal Son, using Acts 3.19 and Luke 15.11–24. It might be especially useful for those only able to have a Family Service once a month, as it does not in any way depend on what has gone before.

I had wanted to speak on the subject of repentance and in the concordance found this text from Acts 3.19: 'Repent . . . and turn again, that your sins may be blotted out. . . . .' On pondering how it might be portrayed, I realized that it was splendidly illustrated by the Prodigal Son in our Lord's famous parable. When the young man came to himself, what did he do? He thought about home, decided to return there and did so, *ie* he changed his mind, which is exactly what repentance means, and he changed his direction, turning round to go home.

As the main text does not come in the story I decided to put it up in letters on a teazlegraph board, with *Repent* and *Turn* emphasized in letters a different colour from all the others. I then constructed in white cardboard a face to represent the Prodigal Son, with a slot at the back into which I could slip another piece of cardboard, on one side of which was the word *God* and on the other side *Self*, as illustrated.

I made a hole in the face where the mouth comes, so that when *Self* was pulled up and seen the mouth looked miserable; but if the card was turned round so that *God* could be seen the mouth looked cheerful. I also constructed a post with two signs that could be fitted into it pointing in different directions, one sign having on it *The Far Country* and the other having on it *The Father's House*.

The talk took the following shape:

I once heard a sermon at a chapel in a Welsh valley that went on for

50 minutes! I was told that if I remembered nothing else about that sermon, I would remember the text, and the preacher was quite right. The text was, 'Ezra stood on a pulpit of wood.' The trouble is, I have not found that text a great help in my Christian life! I hope you will always remember the text that I want to show you this morning, because it could make a tremendous difference to your life. Here it is.

(I got the congregation to read it with me, stressing *Repent* and *Turn*. I then told the story in Acts 3 that led up to those words being spoken by Peter, and repeated the text again.)

What does it mean to repent? Do you remember the story of the son who wanted his share of the money that would come to him when his father died?

(Here I told the story of the Prodigal Son, and how he only thought of himself. I showed him and pulled out his 'thinking' to show the word *Self*, as illustrated above. I talked about how he changed his mind and thought about his father and going home. I took out the card from the back of the face and reversed it, explaining that *repentance* means to change one's mind.)

When we repent we stop thinking about ourselves and we start thinking about God. We ask Him to forgive us for straying from Him. The Prodigal Son turned round and went home, and that is what we have to do as well. We have to stop going into the far country, and turn round and come home to God.

(I illustrated this point in the following way, taking in my case Leeds and Bradford.)

Imagine someone four miles outside Leeds heading for Bradford, asking me how far it was to Leeds. My reply was, '24,996 miles, but if you like to turn round it is only four miles.' I think my enquirer would probably turn round! When we repent and turn, what does the text promise us?

(I got the congregation to read the text again, and someone to pick out the answer to my question. I illustrated it again by the well-known story of John Newton who heard the Gospel very clearly when he was a child, but went away to sea and became the owner of a slave ship, was shipwrecked and brought to his knees before God. He promised that if he was saved he would serve God for the rest of his days, which he did. Like the Prodigal Son, he repented and turned. I quoted the text again, getting the congregation to join in.)

When I used this talk we also had a Baptism. The questions and responses in the Series 2 Baptism Service were very convenient, namely, 'Do you turn to Christ?' 'I turn to Christ.' 'Do you repent of your sins?' 'I repent of my sins.' I challenged the congregation as to whether they had repented and turned, that their sins might be blotted out.

(c) The Christian Family (John 12.1–8)

This is a talk suitable for a special occasion. It could easily be used on Mothering Sunday or on a Family Service Anniversary. In fact, it was the Family Service talk I gave on my final Sunday in my previous parish. I had had the occasion in my mind for some months, and then my former secretary and her husband, one of my churchwardens, requested that their grandson might be baptized on the same occasion, and obviously I was pleased to agree. I prayed much, then when reading Martin Parson's book *Family Life in a Christian Home*,[1] I came across a delightful illustration about family life based on the family at Bethany where Jesus spent many happy hours. It was not long before the following outline took shape:

The Christian Family

Lazarus	Witness	Home
Martha	Worker	Hands
Mary	Worshipper	Heart

An artist in my congregation drew me some delightful figures on white card of Lazarus and his two sisters. She also painted some hands on pink fluorescent paper which I cut out. I drew and cut out a house on orange fluorescent paper and a heart on red fluorescent paper. From my arsenal of teazlegraph letters I put on teazlegraph strips the three words *Witness*, *Worker*, and *Worshipper*. I struck velcro on the back of all the figures and the teazlegraph strips. (The words *The Christian Family* can also be put on the teazlegraph board.) The talk took the following shape:

What is different about the Christian Family? The Bible has much to say about family life and the upbringing of children. (I enlarged on this point.) Jesus knew all about family life: the problem of helping out when Joseph had died, brothers and sisters not understanding Him, and so on. The family I want to look at today just consisted of a brother and two sisters, but each shows us something that goes to make up the Christian family.

[1] Falcon, 1972.

(Reveal the words *The Christian Family* at the top of your board.)

A supper party was planned for Jesus, who of course brought along His disciples. Let us look at each member of the family. (As I referred to the various visual aids I put them up.)

Lazarus the Witness

(Refer to his recent death and his being raised to life by Jesus.) He was a living witness to the power of Jesus, not so much by what he said but just because he was there. This should be true in the Christian home where parents know the power of Christ. Their lives should be a witness. It is what they are that counts just as much as what they say, though of course we must have a reason for the hope that is in us, and be prepared to say so when the occasion arises. Children are to be brought up in the fear and nurture of the Lord, as the Marriage Service says.

Martha the Worker

We are told that Martha served (verse 2).

(I told as vividly as I could the other story of Martha and Mary in Luke 10.38–42, ending with a free paraphrase of her words to Mary, 'You sit there doing nothing while I am working my fingers to the bone,' and Jesus's remarks to her, 'Martha, Martha, you are anxious and troubled about many things.')

Jesus was not rebuking her for doing the work but for being anxious about it. In a Christian family we should all be doing our work for the Lord. I once heard of a woman in London who actually had a notice over her sink, 'Divine Service performed here three times a day.' Adam had work to do before the Fall. The trouble with our fallen world today is not only that some cannot get work, but also that some do not want to work, and do not know how to use their spare time either. In a Christian home all should share in the work. The devil finds work for idle hands to do. In the Christian family children should learn to work heartily to the Lord, and to know Paul's words, 'If a man won't work neither should he eat.'

Mary the Worshipper

(I reminded the congregation about the sweet-smelling ointment that Mary poured over Jesus' feet.)

Mary was a worshipper. She was also the one who sat at Jesus' feet and listened to His teaching. I am sure that Jesus would not have expected Martha to do all the work while Mary just sat at His feet. Hence in one version of the story in Luke 10 we are told that Mary '*also* sat at his feet'. Mary knew that whatever else had to be done one thing must not be omitted, and that was worship, costly worship.

(Refer to the price of the ointment)

What does our worship cost?

(I put up the heart, and referred to grace and family prayers in the Christian home.)

It is quite extraordinary how other things get done when worship is put first. Is yours a Christian family where there is the witness of the home, the work of hands and the worship of hearts?

Note

All three of these talks have been used at services that included a Baptism.

5 The lay person speaking (JT)

There are, of course, many lay people who thoroughly enjoy the opportunity to teach at Family Services, and these are the people who are often used for this ministry. They will, I am sure, benefit from all that is said here in this book, and will be able to adapt and use what has already been written in *Teaching the Families*. However, in every congregation there are those lay folk who, though not prepared to teach regularly in Family Services, have nevertheless a real vital contribution to make, and it is to these people that I want to address myself in this section, being a layman myself.

If you have read as far as this, and have quite firmly decided that speaking at the Family Service is not for you, even if you are asked to do so: then wait a minute. What is a Family Service? Surely the sharing together of worship, experience of God and teaching as a family of God's people. Each of us has something to contribute to that corporate experience of God which would be an encouragement and help. Think again then. If you as a lay person were asked to speak at a Family Service, where would you begin?

Firstly, remember that really to communicate you must be yourself, because communication is essentially to make one's own experience and knowledge part of some other person. You can now forget about imitating Rev. X or Mr Y; that will never communicate your experience. Ask yourself the question, 'In which part of my life does my knowledge of the truth in the Lord Jesus Christ really meet difficulty or opposition, encouragement or joy?' Is it at work on the shop floor or in the office, on the bus or at home with the neighbours? Then these are the things to talk about. Simplicity, directness and the personal testimony are in themselves aids to learning, so you need not be too concerned about elaborate visual aids. A few headings on a magnet board or flannelgraph, or better still the tools of your trade, an illustration of what you do at work or your hobby, will interest all the 'family' in the congregation. Speaking personally about what God means to you, illustrate what you have to say with a few well-chosen Bible verses, and God will richly bless you as He will your audience.

If you are not used to speaking in public, then practise beforehand what you want to say in the place where you are to speak. Get your wife or husband or friend to sit at the back and listen—they will soon say if they can't see or hear well. Doing this will give you the confidence to speak up during the Family Service. Remember, children do fidget and people will cough. Don't be put off by this sort of movement, it is all part of being a family. Remember the noise and movement always seems worse to you in the front than to the rest of the congregation.

4 Family Service development

There may be various reactions to all that has been written in this book so far. Some may be saying, 'It is all very well to suggest a simple Family Service every week, but it would be quite disastrous to impose it on our present congregation. A lot of our people come from the local university and expect much more spiritual nourishment than a weekly Family Service can provide.'

A rather similar plea might come from a parish where the Family Service has been part of the weekly programme for some time, and the question may be asked, 'Can Christian parents continue to live spiritually on a regular diet of Family Service talks, however well prepared and doctrinally orthodox they may be?' In some socially deprived areas this problem may not arise, and in at least one university town where the congregation might be described as intelligent and middle class, a weekly Family Service is happily accepted. However, some parishes may feel the time has come for some changes to be made.

Then some may have inherited a parochial situation where there is a weekly Eucharist to which quite a lot of families come. To attempt to stop it does not seem right, yet it is not the sort of service to which new people, especially unbelievers, can easily be invited. Of course, some situations may demand that Christian parents should be prepared to come to a weekly Family Service, not only for the sake of their children who come with them, but also to encourage those parents who are in the process of finding their way to church for the first time or making their way back after a lapse since Sunday School days. Christian parents who appreciate the importance of this will no doubt be able to find time, either on Sunday evening or mid week, to receive meatier teaching.

However, it is hoped that the ideas in this chapter may suggest ways of dealing with some of these problems, though the precise method will obviously vary according to the particular situation. Whatever is done, however, it is probably both valuable and desirable for most of the family to worship together throughout at least once a month, and also on such occasions as Mothering Sunday, Easter, Harvest and Christmas.

1 All-age instruction
A number of parishes today are developing all-age instruction classes, by means of which graded teaching is provided for the whole family of God from the youngest to the oldest.

Theory
All-age instruction seems clearly to be implied in Scripture: Deutero-
nomy 4.9–10; 6.4–7; 31.7–13; 32.46; Joshua 4.6–7; 2 Chronicles 34.30;
Ezra 7.10; Nehemiah 8.5–8 and Psalm 148.12–13.

To implement such a programme will almost certainly mean radical
restructuring of our normal church services and activities. Charles
Hutchins writes:[1]

'We may have to face the fact that something in the life of the
Church as a whole may have to be dispensed with to make the structure
feasible and workable. Perhaps an organization or all Church organizations would need to close so that everyone could give the necessary
time on a Sunday; it might mean facing a building programme,
with consequent financial implications.

'. . . A structure is needed, a blue print which enables the sights
which have been set to remain clear and attainable. The Scriptures
make it clear that disunity is a mark of carnality (1 Corinthians 3.1–4)
whereas the Holy Spirit brings order out of chaos (Genesis 1.2) and
order should be a sign of the Church (1 Corinthians 14.40). In other
words the Holy Spirit is not opposed to order, rather he works through
it. It is not good enough just to limp on, and, though the whole cannot be reached overnight, we cannot afford to waste precious time—we
must get on with the task before us. Perhaps it is not as easy to bring
to birth a full Christian Education programme in the Church of
England as in other denominations because of the set liturgy, but that
doesn't absolve us from the responsibility of trying.

'What sort of structure do we envisage? Certainly the best is one
which enables all ages to meet at the same time and receive instruction
at their own level. This is best achieved in the mornings, though the
buildings available and the time factor will determine the details.
Teaching must be linked with worship in some way—and the best
arrangement is surely when the worship leads out of the instruction.
Sunday, being the first day of the week and the day on which the early
Christians celebrated the resurrection, has been the traditional day for
the Christians to meet for worship. Modern sociological trends have
meant greater mobility for people, and hence Sunday afternoons are
used for family outings. Obviously the evening is not the best time
to be bringing youngsters and babes in arms, which leaves the morning.

[1] *Teaching in the context of worship* (Grove Booklet on Ministry and Worship
No. 11).

There is nothing, of course, to prevent instruction taking place on a weekday (in many places it supplants Sunday teaching) but if the teaching is to be related to worship in any dynamic way, then it is clearly the Sunday morning structure we need to examine.'

Essential requirements

1 *Adequate premises* are perhaps the primary need. Frequently Anglican churches come off worse here. If space is very limited, young people aged 13–18 are probably the group that could most easily be housed elsewhere, though still involved in the scheme. Derek Osborne writes from Cromer about his all-age programme 'Ten-to-Ten':

'Ideally the Pathfinder age group should meet with the others, in the same building, but we just don't have enough room in our Parish Hall for this, so our Pathfinders meet separately in the Town Youth Centre, though we think of them all as being 'Ten-to-Ten''.

Teenagers like a measure of independence so this arrangement helps provide it. St Faith's Church in Maidstone, which has its main church in the town and a daughter church on a housing estate, ferries a junior Church to the main building by car each Sunday to overcome the premises problem.

2 *Teaching staff* are the next requirement. Here we have a tremendous opportunity to use our laity. Derek Osborne writes:

'We have brought together for "Ten-to-Ten" a group of Church members who are all new to teaching, except for one or two, but they have shown tremendous enthusiasm, and they meet together every month to plan ahead the lessons, etc. for the following month, and to pray together. They have also benefited from some training sessions with Paul Oliver of Scripture Union.'

Tony Thompson in Otley has three laymen who regularly teach the adults. This means that not only can he be freed from time to time to take a children's class, but also can occasionally accept an invitation to preach elsewhere.

It is obviously important that the teachers themselves get adequate spiritual nourishment. David Pawson (a Baptist minister in Guildford) gives the instruction he will be imparting to the adults on Sunday to the teachers earlier in the week, so that they in turn can adapt the teaching to the age level of the children or young people in their classes. Other churches make sure there is adequate provision for teachers either on Sunday evening or during the week. Some aim to change teachers after one or two years, so that a larger number of the adults share in the teaching ministry to the children of the congregation.

In my present church we now have a regular Tuesday instruction meeting when the person preaching in church on the Sunday morning gives his sermon to the Sunday School teachers and Bible class leaders, so that they do not miss their own instruction and also receive help from the staff in preparing their own lessons. We work 12 days in advance to allow teachers plenty of time in their preparation, and we use the talents of former RE teachers in the congregation who no longer teach because (for example) they have families of their own. The fact that the staff now have to prepare their sermons some while in advance was initially somewhat of an ordeal for them, but they now very much welcome it—to have to present one's message to an audience before helps to reveal any shortcomings, which can then be rectified before it is presented to the main congregation.

3 *Teaching materials* are obviously very important. Several churches known to me use Scripture Press (the main criticism of this being that it is very American). This organization publishes a useful booklet by the Rev. Andrew D. MacRae entitled *All-Age Christian Education*. For practical comments on this system of teaching, one correspondent writes as follows:

'The teacher's book is excellent, giving clear teaching to the teacher. For fives to sevens we use visual aid packs and pupil activity packs. For Explorers, visual aid packs and pupil work books. For Pathfinders, visual aid packs plus take-home-papers.

'We find we have to prune things a bit in order to fit the lesson into forty minutes.

'With the adults we use the adult syllabus. The adult magazine for the students is available. Roughly one-third of our adults buy this each quarter. A number testify to the blessing that these are. There are daily readings and explanation on the theme for the coming Sunday.'

Some churches produce their own syllabi. The one outlined in Appendix B was worked out to cover each section of the historical parts of the Old and New Testament, alternating each, but taking them more or less in chronological order. I know that in recent years the thematic approach has been popular with educationalists, but I believe it has been at the cost of the children not getting a real grasp of the Bible story. If parents have really grasped that they are responsible for the Christian upbringing of their children, then they will make a real effort to supplement what their children learn in classes.

Large sections of the more difficult parts of Scripture are not included in the Syllabus, but adults will have plenty of opportunity to get instruction on those sections on other occasions in the total parish programme.

4 *Programme*. Every parish is so different that it would be impossible to legislate, but certain principles need to be considered. Personally I believe there is much to commend having the instruction first, as Charles Hutchins says: 'The best arrangement is surely when worship leads out of instruction.'

Michael Wilcock, Vicar of St Faith's, Maidstone, writes:

'After a hymn, notices, and a pulpit prayer, comes the sermon. This reversal of the traditional order is one of our major innovations.

'Reversal of order: the choice of readings, hymns, etc., previously either meaningless or at best a puzzle ("What is this service about? What's the connection between its parts?") is now seen to fall into place and illuminate (we hope) the main message of the week.'

So, when we set about reordering our Morning Worship at my present church we aimed to achieve the following objectives (which are to some extent interdependent of each other):

(i)   To make it more family-orientated, yet without spoiling Morning Worship for those without families.

(ii)   To make the worship arise more naturally from the instruction imparted—hence the instruction comes first.

(iii)   To attempt to impart teaching from the same passage of Scripture to the whole congregation, including whole family units, but at a level appropriate to age.

Our Sunday morning arrangements are as follows:

First Sunday of the month—Family Service
For some time this has been a tradition. It goes well, attracts new people including students who would be unlikely to come to anything more formal, and provides a Sunday when teachers do not have to teach and so can slip home if, say, parents live outside the city. The uniformed organizations parade and there is a good family atmosphere. Only children under $3\frac{1}{2}$ do not come into church.

2nd and 4th Sundays of the month
On arrival at church, all those under 18 go straight to their own classes, and those over 18 come into the main worship area of the church. After very shortened Morning Prayer (Confession, Absolution, Psalm and Old Testament Lesson, Canticle or hymn and second lesson) the All-age Instruction is given, sometimes illustrated by

means of the overhead projector for headings, maps, etc. This is followed by the Creed. A bell is rung 45 minutes after the beginning of the
service in all places where instruction is taking place, and all the children
over 3½ come into church with their teachers and join their parents.

I personally believe that the children who come without parents
should be sent home after the graded instruction and their parents
told why. It is psychologically bad for parents who may have come
reluctantly to the All-age Instruction to find that there is a group of
children all sitting together with Sunday School teachers. These
parents would soon get the idea that they need not come and could
let their children join the parentless group.

The organist plays some suitable music while the children join us,
which helps to create a worshipful atmosphere. The remainder of
the programme consists of: a hymn; a special item (which may be
a quiz between adults and children, an interview, or even a baptism);
some choruses from Family Worship; the prayers that follow are
taken by a variety of people. One week it may be a family, another a
section of the Sunday School, or a member of staff, or mature adult.
We pray home some of the lessons from the day's teaching, sing a
final hymn and end with the prayer on the middle of page 9 of *Family
Worship*, followed by the Grace or the Blessing.

3rd (and 5th) Sundays of the month
Holy Communion according to Series 3. Only the oldest children
join the adults after the Creed, and Sunday School teachers can have
longer with the children.

In his book *Evangelism: The Counter Revolution*[1] Lewis Drummond
refers to the Rev. Rodney Collins of London who has built up a fine
example of all-age Bible training in his pastorate. His church buildings
are far from the best. He has had a minimum of trained leadership
flowing into his church. Resources are limited. All he has is vision and
determination, yet now a fine programme of all-age Bible study is a
regular part of the church's life. As Dr Drummond comments, 'If he
can do it in his relatively small, limited church, anyone can.'[2]

[1] Marshall, Morgan and Scott.
[2] Two useful booklets on this subject are *Teaching in the context of Worship*
(Grove booklet No. 11) by Charles Hutchins; and *Christian Education on
Sunday morning* (Grove booklet No. 31) ed. by Charles Hutchins, in which
the earlier development of my own All-age Instruction programme is described,
as well as the experience of three other parishes. Margaret Old also writes
briefly about this subject in *Today's Child, Tomorrow's Church* (Scripture
Union, 1974), pages 93–95.

2 Family Communion

In chapter 2 I pleaded for a Family Service to take the shape of simplified Morning Prayer, and if I was just instituting a Family Service for the first time, in the vast majority of parochial situations I would still think that would be the right way to proceed. However, in some parishes it may be found that after some years of this more conventional Family Service there may be a demand for a Family Communion Service. This was the experience, for example, of Bramcote, Nottingham. After various experiments which failed, the parish began having Holy Communion every Sunday morning except when it held its monthly Family Service. Much to the surprise of the vicar, this service immediately caught on, not merely with families, but also with the older members of the congregation whom he thought would not appreciate this type of worship. This led in turn to the publication of *Series 3 for the Family*.[1]

In other parishes the best that might be done would be to have Holy Communion tacked on to the Family Service, say twice a month, with the Sunday School and crèche continuing until the sacrament is over.

In my present parish on occasions (including Christmas and Easter morning) we have adapted Series 3 Holy Communion. A quiz is held on the two lessons; hymns, choruses, creed and prayers are all taken from *Family Worship* and the Family Service type of talk is given. This has been much appreciated.

Where All-age Instruction has been instituted, Holy Communion might be the normal vehicle for worship on some Sundays of the month. This, of course, could mean that children were sitting with their parents. One would hope that both parents and other adults would accept this, even though it might be found distracting initially, because it would be a real help towards family worship, as those parishes who have held a weekly Parish Communion for years will know. This brings us to the whole thorny question of when children should be allowed to receive the sacrament, which is dealt with in the next chapter.

[1] Notes and arrangements by the Rev. J. J. Hamilton-Brown, vicar of Bramcote. Published by Grove Books, Bramcote, Notts., and also distributed by CPAS.

5 The admission of children to Communion

How soon do we allow children to receive the sacrament, assuming that they are converted and really love the Lord? Do we have to wait until they have been confirmed? This is one of the major problems which the Church of England has to grasp at the moment. The practice in many churches has been that children come up to the Communion rail with their parents and receive a 'priestly pat on the head' from the celebrant while the parents receive the sacrament. I heard of one church that actually gave the children 'unconsecrated' bread to eat, though how they told the difference I could not quite understand!

But if the children are baptized and genuinely believe, why should they not receive the sacrament? On what biblical grounds should they have to wait until they have been confirmed? Would it not be far preferable that, with agreement between the parents and vicar, Christian children should be allowed to receive the bread and wine? This would mean that the whole character of Confirmation would be changed, I believe for the better.

I have felt for some time that to attempt to pump Christian doctrine into young people at the age of about 14, when they are experiencing the traumas of adolescence and possibly very much involved in preparing for 'O 'levels, is mistaken. Far better to wait until they are, say, 16½, when such training can become more of a preparation for adult church membership, and the actual service of Confirmation more an act of commissioning, especially as they are eligible to join the Electoral Roll at the age of 17. Obviously I cannot say that these proposals should be put into practice, because they would be contrary to the present regulations of the Church of England; however, they are among the proposals of the Report of the Commission on Christian Initiation (under the chairmanship of the Bishop of Ely). Paragraph 122 reads as follows:

'Concerning admission to Communion, we recommend that:
1 It be permissible for the parish priest, at his discretion, to admit persons to Communion (if they so desire) who have been baptized with water in the name of the Trinity.
2 Adequate preparation for admission to Communion be provided, and be such as to enable the candidates to participate fully in the Eucharist.
3 The first Communion to be administered, wherever possible, by the Bishop.'

And Paragraph 123 states:

'Many young people have lapsed from church-going because they were persuaded to commit themselves at a deep personal level to something they did not understand, whereas in other spheres of their experience they were dissuaded from making decisions, even of a much simpler, kind on the ground that they were too young. We believe, therefore, that the rite of Confirmation becomes more appropriate when it is administered at a suitable age for individual commitment to Christ and his Church. Accordingly we propose that the rite of Confirmation should be regarded primarily as the commissioning of the fully instructed and responsible Christian adult for the work of ministry and mission in the world to which he is thereby committing himself.'

I put some questions on this subject[1] to the Diocesan Bishops in the Church of England (and three Area Bishops in London), and was gratified to receive some sort of reply from all of them. Only ten stressed that they could not really commit themselves on matters that must be decided by the General Synod (although others may have felt this). To get some idea of how the ultimate vote on the Ely Report may go, it is perhaps worth stating the views of the Bishops in general terms.

Several Bishops mentioned that they were permitting controlled experiments in some parishes within their dioceses. For example, in the Diocese of Southwark experimentation took place in the Eltham area. The Sub-Dean writes in the *Southwark News*, August 1973, as follows:

'In the autumn of 1970 we decided at a Chapter Meeting to ask the Bishop whether he would permit us to admit young people to Communion but defer Confirmation until the age of seventeen. The Bishop gave his approval for the experiment provided the candidates were adequately prepared. As Sub-Dean I wrote to each PCC to ask for its support and in every case it was given. We now had to explain the new policy to our congregations. Not everyone was happy with the experiment. Some felt it was wrong to break with tradition while others pointed out we were getting out of step with the rest of the Church of England. However, to many people the new policy made sense from their own experience of having been confirmed when they were too young.

[1] During 1973.

'We consulted together to draw up a syllabus to cover the preparation which we agreed should take six weeks. We spent a morning at a local school where a member of the Chapter was Head of Religious education, watching modern teaching techniques over closed-circuit television and then later discussing the subject. We compiled a form of admission to be used at the Parish Communion and designed a card to give to the candidates. It read "With the approval of the Bishop N. N. has been admitted to Communion after instruction" and was signed by the Parish Priest. On the back of the card were instructions to the candidate including what to do when attending another church.

'All candidates must first become part of the worshipping community before they are prepared for Communion. We no longer have those whose parents think it is time they are confirmed. We still expect to have some who will lapse because the reasons why young people drift away from church are complex. At least we have something more to offer them by way of instruction and an act of commitment when they return. We tell candidates to tell us if they are to move away from Eltham so that we may commend them to their new parish and explain the situation. It is too early to assess the experiment but it does pastorally make sense and there is not a priest in the sub-deanery who would want to go back to the old system.'

I asked the Bishops if they would be prepared for parish priests in their dioceses, at their discretion, to allow children to receive the sacrament of Holy Communion (if they so desired) provided they had been baptized with water in the name of the Trinity. Twenty-four Bishops were in favour (though some added: on an experimental basis for a limited period) and 15 against. Asked what lower age they would require and what other conditions they would impose, if any, two were prepared to permit children as young as seven to receive, but the average age was nine (an age hinted at in the Ely Report, paragraph 134). Almost all who replied to this question were adamant that this really only applied to those children whose parents (or at least one parent) were fully committed and active members of the church, and that the children came to the sacrament with them.

On the subject of Confirmation, 20 Bishops favoured the rite (whether it retained the name of Confirmation or not) being delayed until about 17, which is the minimum age required before joining the Electoral Roll. In this way, preparation classes could more obviously be regarded as training for adult church membership and Christian service.[1] Five Bishops were quite specifically against this, believing the traditional pattern of Infant Baptism, Confirmation and Communion to be the right one. The late Bishop Guy, then Bishop of Gloucester, did, however, ask the pertinent question, 'And what happens when they reach the mystic age of 17 and decide they still do not want to make this act of irrevocable commitment? Are they to continue as communicants? or be repelled?' One can only assume that if these teenagers reject Confirmation they will most likely not wish to continue as communicants.

Roger Beckwith[2] also discusses this point. He writes:

'If Confirmation were no longer admission to Communion, it would be much harder to persuade people that they needed to be confirmed and Confirmation preparation, to which evangelicals attach so much pastoral and evangelical importance, would cease to have a significant place in the life of the Church.'

One of the Bishops who takes the traditional line to which I have recently referred, but who wishes to remain anonymous, writes most helpfully:

'I believe, as the compilers of the Prayer Book believed, that our Anglican scheme of infant baptism followed by the catechumenate and confirmation at an age of responsible choice and decision, is true to the New Testament understanding of initiation into the Church and is a proper prelude to the receiving of the Holy Communion, which is the way in which the life of the Body of Christ gives itself sacramental expression. I believe it is wrong to say that in the New Testament baptism is the whole means of initiation into the Church. It is correct if the statement includes in baptism personal faith, but infant baptism does not include that.

'The trouble is, in my judgment, that this reasonable sequence of initiation completed before Communion, has been spoilt by certain developments. The first has been the strong pressure on the part of many to have Confirmation at a much earlier age than used to be customary. This arises, of course, partly out of the desire to make children communicants earlier. This pressure, again, arises from an understanding of the Holy Communion which stresses it as an indivi-

---

[1] See Ely Report, paragraph 123, quoted above.
[2] In an essay 'The Age of Admission to Communion', Spring 1971 ed. of *The Churchman*.

dual means of grace and tends to hold to the conviction that unless
this Sacrament is received by someone he is deprived of the grace of
God except in some partial and limited way. There seems to me to be
some stresses in all this which need correction. The custom of children
being brought to the communion rail for a blessing has caused great
confusion of thought. It is often argued that because children who come
for a blessing say they are deprived and want to be communicants
they should therefore be allowed to do so, but there are many things
in family life which are denied to young people until well on in their
teens. . . .

'. . . I think that you are on the right lines in thinking of families.
What we need is a much more complete system of Christian education
in the Church, touching people of all ages, and something which will
hold young people in a Christian fellowship until an age older than
the present average one, when they can come to Confirmation with
some conviction.'

This final point underlines the need for all-age instruction.

Bishop Guy makes the point that the requirements for a communicant at any celebration are exactly the same as those required for
Confirmation, namely:

'Ye that do truly and earnestly repent'
The Creed
The intention 'to lead a new life, following the commandments of
God and walking henceforth in his holy ways.'

He dislikes the unbiblical expression 'commitment' on the grounds
that none of us can make an irrevocable decision for life at, say,
Confirmation. 'We are wrong to ask anybody at any age to see his
Christian life in terms of commitment. It is simply not the right word.
We are sons, not recruits. We do not "sign" for service, we rejoice in
our sonship and in the manifold Grace which God pours upon us.'
I think this is a valuable point, though the military metaphor is a
biblical one and incorporated in the Baptism Service.

Even if the General Synod does accept the proposals of the Ely
Commission, as the views of the Bishops indicate it may, evangelicals
seem to be divided on this issue. Paragraph 74 of the Keele Statement
reads as follows:

'We call for further theological study as to whether the age of discretion is always the right time for admission to Holy Communion.
Some of us would like the children of Christian families to be admitted

as communicants at an early age, provided that there is adequate baptismal discipline.'[1]

Some 'further theological study' has been taking place among evangelicals since then. Colin Buchanan has written on the matter in an article 'An Anglican Evangelical Looks at Sacramental Initiation'.[2] He argues that the age of Confirmation ought to be raised from what it is at present (12–14) to about 16, but that it should be separated from admission to Communion, which should instead be combined with baptism. If this were done, a child of Christian parents who had been baptized as an infant would be 'in principle, admissible to Communion with his parents' (the exact age at which he started to receive being 'at their discretion', however). A child of non-Christian parents, on the other hand, would be baptized only when he or his parents professed faith, and would be admitted to Communion at whatever age the profession was made. He makes a similar case in his chapter *The Church and Baptism* in the book of which he is the editor, *Evangelical Essays on Church and Sacraments* (SPCK).

Roger Beckwith disagrees with Colin Buchanan in the essay in *The Churchman*,[3] and Christopher Byworth[4] comments on various points Roger Beckwith makes. In order to draw out the main issues, it might be helpful to compare the disagreements. Roger Beckwith's arguments are as follows:

1 There is a direct parallel between Passover and the Lord's Supper, and Jews did not partake of the former until they were about 20 years of age.

Christopher Byworth takes issue with this, drawing on information from Jeremias, The Mishnah, Josephus and, of course, Scripture. His views might be summarized in two quotations:

'In the New Testament period, where the Lord's Supper was part of a family meal to start with and held in the home, it is hard to see both why and how the children could have been excluded, at least among Jewish Christians. . . .

'The church must treat the baptized (even young children) as believers, rather than as merely potential believers. If it cannot do this,

[1] See *Keele 67*: The National Evangelical Anglican Congress Statement (Falcon, 1967).

[2] *Faith and Unity*, May 1968.

[3] Spring 1971.

[4] *Communion Confirmation and Commitment* (Grove Booklet on Ministry and Worship No. 8, page 13ff.).

it should not baptize them. If it can do this, it should admit the baptized to communion.'

2   Wine is not a suitable drink for children, and in New Testament days the amount of wine drunk at the Lord's Supper would not be restricted to a mere sip.

To this Christopher Byworth, basing his views on the whole status of children in the Bible, writes that:

'. . . while it is suitable to give an infant a (symbolic) wash, bread and wine are not suitable food and drink. However, the whole objection seems irrelevant, as the congruity of the element is simply not part of the argument in respect of either sacrament.'

3   Whereas in the 3rd century AD there are unmistakable references to infant baptism, and implicit references in earlier writers suggest that the practice goes back at least as far as the late 1st century, the first clear references to Infant Confirmation (and therefore Communion) are of a much later date.

Christopher Byworth replies: 'As the earliest definite evidence of infant baptism is about AD 200, this is hardly a major difference.'

4   Roger Beckwith admits that the age of maturity is not an age which can be rigidly fixed, and the Bible does not attempt to fix it in this way. However, one need not hesitate to say that it is an age which a young child has certainly not reached, and which an adolescent may well not have reached either. He concludes with an important point that has direct bearing on the question of children receiving Holy Communion with their parents:

'Granted that the faith of a child is not mature, it may be said, yet it is nonetheless real and a child of Christian parents is united in a family relationship with those whose faith is both real and mature. This however, though true, is not relevant. A communicant, as we have said, is in sacramental terms a committed and practising Christian: he has therefore dispensed with the need of drawing his qualifications as a Christian from others. But to appeal to the family relationship is to invoke others and to do so here is to do it in a connection in which it is simply not appropriate.'

With Christopher Byworth I would simply say that: 'If the Lord's Supper is truly a means of meeting with and feeding on Christ, then surely we should encourage our children to appreciate and use it as such? If they have need of God's grace at all, how can we deny them this means of grace?'

I have compared Roger Beckwith's views and Christopher Byworth's replies in order to help readers understand some of the arguments. In fairness to Roger Beckwith, he tells me in a letter that he does not feel Christopher Byworth has answered his points at all adequately. He would recommend the following programme:

'All the family (and indeed the individuals not in families, whether adults or children), would be encouraged to come together to the Ante-Communion. They would all therefore hear the same Lessons, which would have to be carefully selected, possibly in a new Lectionary, for the purpose; but there would be no sermon in the Ante-Communion, as this could not equally suit everybody, and would lengthen the total service. After the Ante-Communion, communicant adults would remain in the church for the Communion proper which could begin or end with the sermon, based on the Lessons previously used. This would give a reasonable length of time for classes to be held in adjoining rooms for unconfirmed adults and for children. These classes would similarly be based on the Lessons used in the Ante-Communion, and would basically consist of instruction, though any other activities previously included in the Family Service or the Sunday School class could be added.'

To appreciate to the full the arguments of Messrs. Beckwith, Buchanan and Byworth, readers must obviously read their complete texts, from which I have quoted but a small part. The subject is obviously becoming a crucial one for the Church at this time, especially for those really concerned to reach whole families for Christ and to integrate them into its full sacramental life.

6 The Christian family

1 At home (JT)

In the course of my work I receive many invitations to speak at school Christian groups or youth fellowships, and one subject that frequently recurs is 'Boy/Girl Relationships'. Leaders feel, probably quite rightly, that it is something that must be 'done' regularly. I have no quarrel with this, of course, provided it is treated properly within the right context. Unfortunately, often someone gives a talk on 'being unequally yoked', and in so doing gives the impression that provided a Christian boy marries a Cnristian girl everything will be perfect for ever more. Indeed, worse than this, the impression is often given that if a Christian boy or girl doesn't marry then there is something quite unnatural about them.

The Church has often been as guilty as the world of romanticizing marriage to the point of unreality, and applying quite wrong pressures upon our young people to marry quickly. Any teaching to young people upon relationships that will lead to the permanent relationship of marriage must include a careful appreciation of the necessary adjustments that need to be made by the individuals so that two might become one. Nowhere is this point made more clearly than in the introduction to the marriage service in the Book of Common Prayer: '. . . and therefore (marriage) is not by any to be enterprised nor taken in hand, unadvisedly, lightly or wantonly . . .' At the same time such teaching needs to be positive, pointing to the joys and privileges of a Christian marriage.

It is not the purpose of this chapter to go into any detail on the pressure which all marriages must face, but to concentrate on the particular problems which confront the Christian couple as they enter into marriage and later family life. Many churches today provide preparation classes for young people coming forward for Christian marriage, and this is excellent. However, very few go on to provide the support and care that is as necessary after marriage as before. Indeed, very often the Church is guilty of bringing undue pressures upon the family rather than nurturing it. So often it is expected that a newly married couple will have plenty of time, before the children come along, to run the youth club, liven up the women's work, bring young blood on the church council, etc., etc., without anyone appreciating the time-consuming element of adjustment in early married life or providing within the fellowship for the sharing of problems and pressures. Worse than that, sometimes the young marrieds are asked to work apart from each other in some church activity which requires close affinity to a single young man or girl.

This may well give rise to jealousy which, with the pressures of early married life, can grow quite out of proportion and cause real misery. Real pastoral insight is needed in harnessing the energies and enthusiasm of our young marrieds to the work of the church in a positive way which will aid their growth together.

The absence of real 'family fellowship' within the church can lead our young people to a wrong impression about 'Christian family life'. They see us at our 'Sunday best'—doing the right things, saying the right things. When our young couple have their first major disagreement, they not only have the real difficulty of solving their disagreement, but also the feeling of spiritual failure. 'If we were really Christians we couldn't possibly have shouted at each other.' It is very often this feeling of spiritual defeat which is so hard to bear.

Of course, 'pray about it' is part of the solution, but it is not the only part. The need to share with others, to talk things through, is of equal importance. True 'family fellowship' within the church will allow relationships to develop that will demonstrate how all families have constantly to work their way through problems and difficulties, and will thus provide the sympathetic ear or the shoulder to cry on.

In any discussion on reaching and caring for the family, consideration needs to be given particularly to the mother of very young children. If she has been an active church member she will probably feel isolated and spiritually non-effective when children come along. How important it is to provide an adequate and well-run crèche for our Family Service so that the young mother can be spiritually fed without uneasiness over the welfare of her children.

At the same time, we must realize that the young father will need to give more of his time to the family if his wife's feeling of isolation is not to be aggravated. This again will require pastoral guidance over priorities, and he should not be pressurized into being away from home too often in the week. If we have a large number of young families in our church, then we need to give particular thought to the starting times of evening activities—6.30 for an evening service would be ridiculous in some churches. In a young family the children's bedtime is the one time when, wherever possible, both parents should be present.

As children grow older, parents feel themselves under constant pressure to ensure that their children conform to what they believe is acceptable 'Christian conduct'. This particularly applies to churchgoing. I have often seen parents struggling with youngsters who are complaining bitterly at having to sit through three Bible readings in

Series 3 Communion, or the Canticles in Morning Prayer. If we really think 'family', then we will be catering for the whole church and providing an environment in which every member of the family can be themselves and at ease.

One of the greatest difficulties my wife and I experienced as first-generation Christians was in the setting of standards in a Christian home. Those who have been privileged to have been brought up in a Christian home will not always appreciate the agonies of decision necessary over seemingly very insignificant details. The provision of teaching, meeting and sharing, needs again to be seen as a vital part of the church's ministry of nurturing families.

Many Christian families have experienced the agony of teenage children who seem to reject the faith in which they have been carefully nurtured from childhood. Here again the feeling of spiritual failure on the part of parents can be very deep and disturbing. This is particularly so if a climate of honesty and sharing has not been built up within the church fellowship. On the other hand, parents feel sometimes that they must 'get their child converted' or they have failed. We have known parents travel many miles to Scripture Union missions with the express intention of getting their child converted. Perhaps this highlights our very inadequate theology of childhood within the Church, a factor which is also demonstrated in the debate in the previous chapter on the admission of children to the Lord's Supper. It is little wonder that children rebel against this pressure. For in fact parents are saying to the child: 'You are not good enough for the family, yet we hope you will be one day.' Perhaps as the church begins to think 'family' it will also begin to recapture something of the 'corporate' nature of our faith found throughout Scripture, and swing back from the highly individualistic interpretation of Scripture so popular in many circles. Then I believe the Holy Spirit will enable us to see clearly the spiritual state of the child and his spiritual needs, and equip His church to meet the needs of all joyfully.

John Pridmore has written:[1]

'If the perfect humanity of Jesus was as fully expressed by his childhood as by his adult manhood, then it must be affirmed that there is potentially for every child, at every age, the proper relationship to God suited to his age. This must be said of the child *as he is*. In the here and now of the child's young life there is an appropriate God-

[1] *Crusade*, September 1973.

child relationship. This possibility is demanded by the norm of Jesus's childhood. If you say you can enter a right relationship with God only after some relatively grown-up religious experience, you deny the incarnation, for the one who lived all his life in perfect relationship with God was once a child.'

If this is true, then our teaching and worship programme must recognize this capacity in all the family and reach out to fulfil it.

2 At church (MB)

Dr Coggan's Presidential Address to the York Convocation in 1962 has already been quoted at some length (page 13). He suggested there that in the past there has been a danger of the Church itself, by its multifarious activities for both sexes and different ages, dividing the Christian family rather than uniting it. So we need to consider in this section of the chapter how the Church can encourage Christian families to do things together.

We have already devoted a considerable amount of space in this book to the whole matter of the family worshipping together, so there is no need to say much more on this .Of course, Family Worship presents special difficulties for clergy. However, our family worships together on holiday, and at other times my wife comes with the family. We never insist on our children wearing special 'Sunday' clothes (even though we tend to do so ourselves), as we feel we would rather have them there happy in clothes they prefer than rebellious in clothes we prefer! As they grow into their teens we do not really expect them there at the Morning Service because they have their own Bible Classes, and are quite happy for them to sit with their own friends in the evening. That is the natural age when we should expect some independence, though within fairly clearly defined limits.

Now, apart from worship, what else can we do together as families? We have already talked about having coffee after the service to break down initial natural British reserve, but there is still a sense in which we are on our best behaviour and cannot get to know each other at any depth under these circumstances.

Why should we not organize a social programme that involves the whole family? Every family normally has the problem at week-ends of having to entertain the children, and this frequently involves some little expense; why not get a number of church families to do something together and then conclude the enterprise with a meal together at one of the homes? Provided people go to different homes on different occasions the expense of doing this need not be exorbitant, for everyone has to eat. If some homes are too small for everyone who wants to come, there are the obvious alternatives of going to a house that is big enough, or to the church hall; and everyone can bring something and share it out. It does not take much organization to ensure that everyone does not bring similar items!

This kind of thing is actually happening in our church with some real measure of success, and is having a number of immediately beneficial results. The first is that parents are getting to know each other at a much deeper level. Secondly, a fellowship is being created into which it is very easy to welcome new members because they immediately feel at home. And thirdly (and this is perhaps as important as anything) children meet other children and make friends, and this makes it very much easier to encourage the children to come to church activities with their parents because they know they will meet other children with whom they are already friendly. Here is a list of some of the things the group has done:

Swimming with the family at a local baths followed by tea in one of the family homes.
Barbecue in a group member's garden, coffee and fellowship in the house later.
Hike to a local beauty spot followed by tea at a member's home.
Sunday lunch at one of the homes and perhaps occasionally at the vicarage.
Christmas party at a member's home.

The church as a whole has also organized a family house party. In spite of the cost and the travelling to the Conference Centre, far more wanted to come than could be accommodated, and it was voted a great success and is to be repeated as soon as the Conference Centre is available again.

Another parish arranges two main family events in the year. The vicar describes them as follows:

'In November (to coincide with our Anniversary) we have a Family Evening of homespun entertainment—fun and games for the children—a "pooled" tea, films and slides of church happenings over the past year (this is normally on the Saturday night, say from 5 pm to 8 pm).

'In June or July we have a Family Day. This takes place in the afternoon and early evening and is roughly as follows:

(a) No fund raising, just a nominal 5p to cover expenses (children free).

(b) Held on the cricket field behind the church.

(c) Children's races and sports—obstacle races for grown-ups, tug-of-war for all—skittles, side shows, donkeys, ices, etc., followed by bring-your-own, pooled tea in the hall, church garden or on the field—after tea a few more stunts and games, and then an annual cricket match between the menfolk, my XI versus the sidesmen or what-have-you. During the afternoon we have a large-scale exhibition of things made during the year by church members—paintings, pottery, etc., and for every age level. We also have cake competitions, flower arranging competitions, etc., and nominal prizes are given out. The catering is in the hands of our 51 fellowship (young grans) who gladly help and probably would not otherwise come, as they would feel out of it with so many young families. We do not make a meal out of either family event—a minimum of planning and prior meetings. The main idea being no agonies, no wasting of valuable man hours—no one debarred because of cost.

'This year 23 of us have been for a week in the Holy Land—youngest 21, oldest 82, so in the evening we are holding a reunion to which everyone is invited—showing two ciné films and slides, etc.'

With the next two suggestions I am 'kite flying', but hope to attempt to put them into operation when the facilities are right. Firstly, a family evening from time to time, possibly weekly or monthly, which starts with a meal together at church at, say 6.30 pm, and then various age groups can break up and 'do their own thing.' Adults can have Bible Study and Prayer Meeting, children could have the sort of activities normally arranged by churches for the different age groups such as Pathfinders, Covenanters, etc., but all arranged to end reasonably early so that the family can go home together.

Secondly, activities on Sunday afternoon for those who are not obliged to visit or entertain relatives. This could start with lunch together after Morning Service and then there might be some games, mental or physical[1], or even a walk if the church is suitably situated. Alternatively, the afternoon activity could begin at, say, 3.30 pm, leading up to tea, after which those with very young children could

[1] Ideas can be found in *Games Galore* and *Ideas Galore* compiled by Patrick Goodland (Scripture Union).

go home. Older children could stay on with their parents for the evening worship and, of course, if the morning programme had been along the lines of all-age instruction, the evening worship could take some entirely new shape with something designed to appeal to all age groups.

Obviously all parishes are different, and some of the ideas suggested above will have to be adapted to suit the prevailing cultural patterns. None of these activities need be exclusively for families, and care must be taken not to make single members of the church feel unwanted—extra 'aunts' and 'uncles' are usually welcome! There will also have to be some fellowship in age groups, and recreational activities for young people. The main thing is that we start thinking in terms of the family enjoying Christian fellowship together, so that no one has to say, as a very keen Christian member of my congregation said to me: 'I come to church for worship and instruction, but my family and I have to find our social life elsewhere.'

In his book *Evangelism: The Counter Revolution*[1] Lewis Drummond says that one of the reasons for a breakdown in communication, especially of the gospel, is a breakdown in community. Dr Drummond suggests this should be met by the creation of a new Christian community through which Christ can be proclaimed. The development of fellowship as families, then, is not only important for its own sake, but also as part of our evangelism.

[1] Marshall Morgan and Scott. See particularly pages 138–139.

7 Evangelizing the family

In its report on family worship, the Keele Conference stated:

'Care must be taken lest this form of evangelism become child orientated and teaching consequently childish. The church must labour in family evangelism as well as in child evangelism, although we recognize the importance of the systematic instruction of children. Further the distinction between adult and child, old and young in the light of the church must not be too rigid. Christian fellowship objectively expressed and fostered through liturgy should break down barriers of age and should unite whole families more securely.'

Mary Alice Jones writes:

'If the church is to fulfil its mission today it must so speak that men and women living in the present world can listen with growing alertness to God as He speaks directly to their own condition. The church can prepare the way for this experience so that persons young and old alike of all nations and cultures and conditions may hear the ancient gospel as the living word today. There is not a children's God and a children's gospel and another for adults and one in between for teenagers. There is not a God and a gospel for our country and another for Africa or Russia. God is God and the gospel is the gospel.'[1]

If, as we have discovered in the previous chapters, God's basic unit is the family, and if what Mary Alice Jones says is also true, then perhaps we need fundamentally to reconsider our whole strategy of evangelism. All of us who are concerned with evangelism need to put to ourselves the question posed by Dr Coggan: 'Is it possible that we, who believe so profoundly in the institution of the Christian Family, and who speak often and vehemently about it, are, by the very form which our church work takes, not helping—perhaps even hindering—that for which we stand' (see page 13). Are the actual 'structures' within our church fellowship militating against the processes of evangelism upon which we have embarked? We can never hope to evangelize effectively if we as a family of God fail to foster the very ideals of relationships within the fellowship outlined in chapter 1.

When dealing with non-Christian families and children from non-Christian homes, we need to understand first of all the strength of home ties upon the small family unit that now exists, and the way in which this home unit will particularly influence the children. Although fallen and far from ideal, that family unit reflects in part the relationships

[1] *Parents, Children and the Christian Faith* (Fontana, 1967).

which God created and expected of man; thus the strength of the
relationship between husband/wife and parent/child must never be
underestimated.

In our children's evangelism and teaching we have been concerned
to bring children to a knowledge of the Lord Jesus Christ, but I
believe that we have not paid sufficient attention to the conflicts
which seeking to bring children to a decision for Christ can cause
within the home. If we are to continue our ministry to the child in the
increasingly secular society in which we live, we need to pay far more
attention to the unit of family than to the individual child.

In her book *Conjoint Family Therapy*,[1] Virginia Satir has a lot to say
about the effects upon the family of one person who appears to be
acting contrary to what is a generally accepted manner of behaviour
within the family. She says, 'When one person in a family has a pain
which shows up in symptoms, all family members are feeling this
pain in some way. The family acts so as to achieve a balance in relationships and members help to maintain this balance either overtly
or covertly. The family's repetitious, circular, predictable communication pattern reveals this balance.

'A growing body of clinical observation has pointed to the conclu-
sion that family therapy must be orientated to the family as a whole.
This conviction was initially supported by observations showing how
family members labelled a schizophrenic. Further studies showed that
families with a delinquent member respond in similar ways to the
individual treatment of this member.'

She goes on to point out that if one member of the family acts in an
unusual manner then all the relationships within the family are affected;
and the family tends automatically (either consciously or unconsci-
ously) to dominate the one member who is acting differently so that
he or she might be restored to the fold or to the normal pattern of
behaviour within that family. Thus changes in patterns of behaviour
fundamentally affect family relationships. If a child is converted to
Christ and produces a different behaviour pattern, this can result
within the non-Christian family in rejection of that child, or in
increasing pressure to normalize or stabilize relationships by making
him revert to his previous role.

Is it possible for a young child converted from a non-Christian
home, or making a profession of faith in Sunday School or evangelistic
meeting, to stand against these very great pressures from within his

[1] Science and Behavior books rev. 1967.

home? Is it right to call a child to make a commitment to Christ in circumstances which will place him in an unbearable position within his home, unless we have taken steps to ensure that the home environment is prepared to receive that child and to understand what has happened? If we are to accept that one effective pattern of evangelism is to work with families, then we must attempt to analyse practically how this might be achieved.

Of course, not all our church members are physically 'in families'. The single men and women making homes for themselves away from their families, or living with old parents or other relatives, are equally church members with a vital role to play. In all our talk about families we must never lose sight of the one family relationship of all God's people within the fellowship of the church. There is a vital evangelistic work to be done among students, in 'bedsitter land', with the old and lonely, and indeed with families, which could well best be left to a single person who has the gift and the time to 'draw alongside'. However, in this book we are primarily concerned with the natural family, though in reaching that we may reach others.

Existing bridges

In his book *Like a Mighty Army*,[1] Maurice Wood refers to an occasion when his unit, the Royal Marine Commandos, had to cross a river in France at Pont l'Eveque:

'It looked as though we were going to have to swim it at night, because there was only one bridge, and that was reduced to a twisted steel girder with fires blazing at one end of it and with the enemy shelling the approach to it. Our commanding officer felt, however, that as it was a bridge it had better be crossed before we attempted the more difficult action of swimming a river whose depth and speed were unknown to us, and whose far bank was studded with mines. We captured that bridge and the whole Commando got across. It was a tenuous link with the other side, but strategically it was the right thing to do. In just the same way there are certain tenuous links between the great mass of people in our country who are otherwise completely out of touch with organized religion. These links must be made stronger and these bridges must be crossed.'

The Christian Church has a number of existing bridges between itself and secular man, especially related to the family.

[1] Marshall, Morgan and Scott, 1955.

1 *The Christian family*
The importance of an established open Christian home in God's plan
of evangelism cannot be overestimated. Dr Martyn Lloyd-Jones says,[1]
'I believe that Christian parents and children, Christian families,
have a unique opportunity of witnessing to the world at this present
time by just being different. We can be true evangelists by showing
this discipline, this law and order, this true relationship between
parents and children. We may be the means under God's hand of
bringing many to a knowledge of the Truth.'

Perhaps far more of our training for evangelism may need to take
the form of training and nurturing the Christian families in our
congregation to take the opportunities of evangelism which are open
to them. For the minister and leaders of the church, this means an
immediate realization that, as has been stated elsewhere, Christian
marriages and Christian homes do have problems and tensions that
require pastoral care, as much as the bright-eyed young things coming
to vestry hour to arrange their forthcoming marriage. Some churches
are good at arranging preparation classes for marriage, but few see
the great need of continuing to provide pastoral help and care, or
even a meeting place for Christian families for the next 5, 10 or 20
years. Statistics show that well over half the divorces occur among
couples whose marriage has lasted 10 years or more. If we are really
concerned to encourage Christian families to be evangelists in their
own right, then as a church we should nurture and care for them as
our most valuable possessions.

A meeting point
The Christian family living a full and active life in society comes into
contact day by day with many other families. It is across these natural
bridges of friendship that we need to bring other families into the
fellowship of the church. The neighbours with whom we go to the
swimming baths or to the park, school, shops or local entertainment
are those whom God has given to us as our special responsibility for
Him. Some of your may have seen the old film *The Gospel Blimp*
or read the book. The rather corny but nevertheless vital truth behind
the story was that we do not win our neighbours for Christ by bom-
barding them with texts but by caring for them as people.

Use of the home
More and more today people are seeking the 'listening ear', the person

[1] *Life in the Spirit* (Banner of Truth, page 240).

or people who are sufficiently concerned to disturb their own programme in order to give time for others. This seems to be true in whatever area we live. Margaret Warde[1] tells how 16 different homes are used by God for evangelism, and deals with some of the practical difficulties of an 'open home'. We need to remember, however, that the 'open home' is a family affair. It may be very helpful for my wife to talk over a neighbour's problem with her during the morning and to become a close confidante, but if I never meet the husband or as a family we don't meet the family together, we are little nearer our goal of family evangelism and nurturing.

Visiting
We need not, of course, sit still and wait for our neighbours to come to us. A birth or a death, problems and joys in the neighbourhood, are good enough reasons for calling and for actively building bridges of friendship. We need not wait for the minister to visit first; if the need is there then our responsibility is to meet it.

Home meetings
Sometimes to lay on a particular function can be a useful way of building bridges with one's neighbours, especially in suburban parishes. A Christian book party to which parents and children together can be invited is one way of getting to know people, and of course of introducing them to the excellent range of Christian books available for all ages today. A gathering to meet an interesting missionary or other visitor to the neighbourhood can be another family affair. If one is contemplating an evening meeting or home Bible study, it is good to try to encourage both husband and wife to attend, and a good-neighbour baby-sitting service for the evening would be one way of achieving this (though this is not always acceptable in some places).

It is important to notice that in some areas people do not naturally visit other people's homes except to drop into the kitchen for a cup of tea. Visiting for the evening is just not part of the way of life. However, often in these areas people are prepared to go out with others to a neutral venue. Working-men's clubs are 'big business' in such areas, often holding 2,000 to 3,000 people on a Friday or Saturday night. It could be possible to organize a 'home meeting' type of programme, but holding it in the local community centre or

[1] *Take My Home* (Scripture Union, 1969).

library, hiring a small room and encouraging church families to come along and bring neighbours.

Hospitality
One of the most natural places for conversation and friendship is a meal together. To invite the neighbours for lunch or tea after an outing is so natural. This provides an excellent opportunity to talk about spiritual things in a completely natural way. Grace at meals, the contents of the bookshelf, the sort of magazines lying around, the way the family is orientated, all point our neighbours to the fact that the head of our household is the unseen Christ. What more natural thing than to invite our friends to join us at church, especially if there is a Family Service, and then return for Sunday lunch together.

When we have built bridges of friendship and brought our neighbours to a Family Service, the tremendous responsibility for continuing to build bridges of friendship now rests with the whole family of the church.

2 Marriage (MB)
Although the church cannot compel those who use its premises for marriage to worship regularly either before or after the wedding, yet strong hints can be dropped about the Family Service, especially if marriage preparation classes are held. Some churches read banns during the Family Service and encourage engaged couples to come. There is much to commend this from the point of view of the engaged couples, especially if they are intending to settle in a parish where there is a Family Service. However, we also need to consider the matter from the point of view of the children. If there are a lot of banns, these can prolong the service considerably and be very boring. Besides, these banns can be very mysterious to children, as in the case of the child who asked his mother who George Augustus Peppermint was whom the vicar thought somebody might know. (Apparently the vicar was not very clear in his pronounciation of 'cause or just impediment.'!) Perhaps the best compromise is to attempt to space the banns out evenly through the permitted period of 12 weeks so that there are never very many at a time, and to read them when younger children are out of the church in classes.

3 Thanksgiving for the birth of a child
Being such a short service, this can conveniently be fitted in after Family Service and before any subsequent service; hence, when a

Churching is requested, we can suggest that both parents come to the Family Service and that the Churching will follow it, perhaps in a chapel attached to the church.

4 Funerals

A visit to a house where there has been a bereavement often produces good opportunities to talk about the living Christ, which in turn may bring promises to attend church. Here again, if the people concerned have long been estranged from the things of God, the simplicity of a Family Service could be just the service for them.

5 Infant Baptism

I mentioned in chapter 1 that one of the factors leading to my development of a Family Service was the need for a service to help parents who were wishing to have their babies baptized become regular worshippers. This inevitably raises the whole controversial subject of so-called 'indiscriminate baptism' on which space allows me to make only limited comment. (Readers are asked to refer to Appendix C for further reading on this subject.)

Those who accept Covenant theology on the subject of Baptism would probably make the following main points: first that the provision of godparents is non-biblical, although no doubt an admirable institution when parents are likely to die young or be thrown to the lions. Secondly, God's basic unit is the family. Just as children enjoy the physical and material privileges of their parents, so they do spiritually. Isaac, therefore, although only eight days old and quite obviously incapable of any personal response to God, yet received circumcision, the sign and seal that he was in a covenant relationship with God because of the faith of his father Abraham. Likewise in the New Testament, where parents become Christian believers their children are regarded as holy and, with their parents, considered fit recipients of the Christian sign and seal of faith which is Baptism.

Over the course of many years, maladministration of Baptism (that is, Baptism of infants where there has been no evidence at all of the Christian standing of the parents) has brought the doctrine of Infant Baptism into disrepute, and even into open question. Some people have attempted to remedy the situation by making the actual Baptism service an 'evangelistic occasion', arguing that since Baptism is a sacrament of the gospel it should be available to all. Personally, I have rarely found the Baptism service an ideal occasion for declaring the gospel to unbelievers—they are unfamiliar with the church, slightly uncomfortable just because the surroundings are strange, very conscious of their relatives and friends who are there, of the clothes especially purchased for the occasion, and of the celebrations shortly to follow the service. It is also more than likely that the subject of the Baptism will cause considerable disturbance!

Further, I would ask what practical evidence there is over the years that this free-for-all has been justified. As the Rev. J. A. Motyer says, 'Are our churches filled with glad converts of sacramental evangelism? Is it not rather the case that such a convert is the exception and not the rule, and that in many—if not most—churches where this justification is urged there is not a single positive evidence of its fruitfulness? Indeed, the ill-fruits of the practice are the evident things . . . a practice is being advocated on evangelistic and pastoral grounds which, in fact, confuses people's minds as to the real nature of the gospel and deludes them into thinking that their status before God is in some way beneficially secured for them when in point of fact they are still in their sins. A curious evangelistic opportunity, this!'[1]

In implementing a strict parochial Baptism discipline, some people fear it will cause unnecessary hostility. It will certainly cause hostility, but whether this is unnecessary is highly questionable. Much of the hostility nowadays is caused because the discipline is not general throughout the country, though the situation is improving. It is understandable that unconverted parents should object when one vicar says the baptism of their baby should be postponed whereas the vicar of a neighbouring parish baptizes without question. A diocesan policy such as that being developed in the Chelmsford Diocese is surely an important lead in the right direction.

Hostility is also caused because the mother feels something is being denied to her baby, and in the highly emotional state that is quite normal after childbirth, tends to fight for her baby's supposed rights and is therefore less open to logic than she might be otherwise. Yet another cause for hostility can be that parents are only too well aware the church is right to refuse when there are no links with it. I have actually had a woman say to me, 'The reason I get so cross with you is because I know you are right.'

However, there are other considerations. We who are clergy need to ask ourselves very seriously whether we adopt a slack baptismal policy, not because we believe it to be right, but because we are

[1] J. A. Motyer, *Paedo-Scandalism*, Church of England Newspaper, 7 February 1964.

literally afraid of the hostility. We like men to speak well of us, but Jesus our Master warns us, 'Beware when all men speak well of you'. As far back as 1907 the Rev. Roland Allen, one-time missionary on the staff of the Society for the Propagation of the Gospel, resigned his living at Chalfont St Peter on this very issue.[1]

I have discovered from personal experience that there are very real gains from a strict baptismal policy. It will bring some people right into the Christian Church—not just as pew-fillers, but as people who come to a personal faith in Jesus Christ. They will have an especial respect for the Church because it was prepared to have the courage of its convictions.

Further, it will make the whole local church aware that there is a cost to Christianity, and that the vicar is prepared to experience part of that cost, for the hostility of a baptism policy will fall chiefly on him.

Finally, it will help greatly in the whole issue of Christian unity, for one of the stumbling blocks to unity with those denominations that do not practise Infant Baptism is the maladministration in the Church of England.

There remains the problem of deciding which babies are eligible for Christian baptism. The simple answer is: those who have at least one parent a real Christian (see 1 Corinthians 7.14). But how are we to decide that? Ultimately we cannot, for God alone knows the hearts of men and women, yet the Lord does say that by men's fruits we shall know them. I believe that real Christians have a kind of sixth sense in this matter. Even so, that cannot be explained to those who are not Christians. There ought to be some reasonable minimum requirements, and the following seem basic:

(i) Church attendance

The church where the baptism is to take place would not be standing if some did not come. Public worship was clearly practised by Jesus and His followers in the New Testament. We are told not to forsake gathering ourselves together. The big problem in expecting church attendance is so often that there is no service suitable for parents, who wish to take the Baptism of their children seriously, to attend. This is where the Family Service comes in. I can think of quite a number of cases where I was able to invite people inquiring about

[1] See *The Ministry of the Spirit*, selected writing of Roland Allen, edited by David Paton (World Dominion Press, 1960), pages 193ff.

Baptism for their children, to attend the Family Service before proceeding any further. They came, they were converted and found a spiritual home, both for themselves and their children. Infant Baptism becomes a meaningful proposition when this happens. Had I not operated a strict policy but proceeded with the Baptism before requiring attendance at the Family Service, I personally doubt whether those families would be anywhere spiritually now.

(ii) Confirmation

Parents who wish to have their babies baptized should presumably be wanting their children one day to be confirmed and become full members of the church. It is logical therefore that they themselves ought already to be full church members. But how can those with little contact with the church suddenly be ready for confirmation classes? This is exactly where the Family Service comes into its own. Again and again I have seen adults awakened to the importance of spiritual things as a result of worshipping in this simple way with their families. Indeed, I have recruited more of my candidates[1] from the Family Service than from any other source. Thus they graduate from Family Service to the full communicant life of the church.

[1] Of course, if Family Service is bright and clear and has a high quality of preparation, Confirmation classes must be equally interesting. Soundstrips and tape-recordings can be used to liven them up: Appendix C gives a number of suggestions.

8 Going on to maturity

At a conference about Family Worship, several clergy said to me that they had good congregations of families coming to church, but there did not seem to be much progress in the lives of the people coming. Quite rightly, they were dissatisfied. Our goal should be to present every man mature in Christ (Colossians 1.28). In this chapter we are concerned with ways of achieving this.

1 Pastoral care

One of the Bible's most used metaphors is that of the shepherd and the sheep. Jesus applied this metaphor to Himself in detail in John 10. He was the 'good shepherd' (verse 11), the 'door of the sheep' (verse 7), the one who knows intimately the members of his flock (verse 14), the one who does not flee when he sees the wolf coming (verse 12), the one who voluntarily 'lays down his life for the sheep' (verse 11).

To those who heard Jesus, little explanation was needed. The Jews were steeped in knowledge of the pastoral life. Most of the great leaders had been shepherds—Abel, Abraham, Isaac, Jacob, Moses, David and so on. Even God Himself is referred to in the Bible as a great Shepherd. National and religious leaders were under-shepherds either caring for or neglecting the Lord's flock, the children of Israel.

The eastern shepherd pursued, and still pursues, an exacting calling He may often have had only a tent to live in. A shepherd on duty was liable to make restitution for any sheep lost (see Genesis 31.39), unless he could really prove the situation was beyond his control or foresight. Shepherds had to be strong, devoted and selfless.

Eastern sheepfolds are walled enclosures with a narrow slit. The sheep are led into the enclosure and the porter guards the door all night for the shepherd. When the shepherd returns in the morning he is let in because he comes by the door. He loves his sheep and knows them all individually. A humble shepherd who cannot afford a porter looks after his sheep himself at night by lying down in the narrow slit of the doorway into the fold so that he will be disturbed by an intruder. The good shepherd leads his sheep rather than driving them. He must find grass and water in a dry and stony land, protect his sheep from weather and wolves, and retrieve any animals that have strayed, even though he may have to go far from home and security himself. The shepherd knows the way, knows the dangers to be avoided, and so leads his sheep to succulent green pastures where they can feed.

The appropriateness of this pastoral metaphor to Christian ministers will be obvious, but before thinking about this let us make two observations about our Lord in the role of the Good Shepherd.

The first is His obedience to His Father (John 10.17, 18). We who are under-shepherds must realize we are under the authority of the Chief Shepherd, the one Peter called the Shepherd and Bishop of our souls.

The second is His loving care for His sheep even to the point of death (John 10,11, 15, 17–18): in His case His death was the most important thing He could do for His sheep. He was the Lamb of God taking the sin of the world.

The nature of pastoral work

What does this biblical teaching mean for those of us involved in pastoral work?

First, we ourselves must, obviously, be within the fold and obedient to the leadership of our Lord.

Second, it must be our primary ambition to lead sheep to Him, who alone gives life.

Third, we must care for the sheep. This will mean knowing them individually by name and visiting them, leading them by the example of our lives, feeding them by teaching them the Word of God, the Bible, and encouraging them to read it themselves. How often the Lord had to rebuke the religious leaders of His day for not knowing the Scriptures! That must never be true of us!

We shall often have to remind ourselves that sheep are prone to straying and that we shall have to go after them time and time again. Caring for our sheep will involve guarding them against wolves, that is, heretical teachers (see Acts 20.28–31). The task is a daunting one, and it is only as we ourselves are listening to the Shepherd's voice and letting Him lead that we can be made equal to it.

Pastoral work in practice

1 Patience

We shall need to be very patient with those we are seeking to attract to the Family Service. This means that a real effort must be made to see the problem of returning to regular church attendance from the point of view of those actually taking the step. For them it means a real family upheaval to get themselves up and the children washed and dressed and fed, including perhaps a baby as well, and to be at church possibly as early as 10 am. Furthermore, newcomers will be very much aware of the neighbours seeing this strange phenomenon of churchgoing, and they will, no doubt, have to face quite a lot of ridicule if they persist in it. Adult church life to them is very mysterious.

We need to go out of our way to be really helpful to these people, and not to be critical if it takes some time for their church attendance to become regular.

2   Division of labour

Though, as has been said earlier, we want to avoid the danger of splitting up the family, yet in providing pastoral care for the family there seems to be real value in a division of labour. One man such as the vicar or pastor cannot keep in personal touch with the many people who eventually attend Family Service. I would suggest the following:

Adults

Gradually we should be aware that various families are becoming very familiar to us and will have heard the Word of God proclaimed week after week during the Family Service. We should now be 'drawing in the net', and this will probably be best done in the home, either by the full-time staff of the church or by mature Christian laity. Someone must visit, and if the season is right, lead those adults in which the Word has been sown to Christ Himself.

Children

The time available for the minister to visit his flock is extremely small, because most people are out during the day, and evenings are often tied up with instruction classes, council meetings, etc.; so some visiting must be delegated.

It was earlier pointed out that in Sunday School the spirit-filled teacher can really get to know his children. These are therefore the most natural people to utilize in the pastoral care of the children who attend Family Service, from 3 years old until they leave to join other groups at around 11 or 12. These teachers should know their children well from the classes, and when visiting their homes will get to know the whole family. Special occasions in the year such as Christmas, Harvest, Anniversary or Prizegiving, will give natural opportunities for visiting, and enough time should be taken to ensure that these visits are not rushed.[1] More and more organizations producing

---

[1] It was significant to read in *A Survey of ten Sunday Schools in the Leeds district of the Methodist Church* by Ivan Reid, 'No Sunday School appeared to have any systematic face to face contact with the parents of children, particularly those who did not attend Church.' Small wonder that the general trend was declining attendances.

material for Sunday School lessons also produce take-home literature, such as the Scripture Union *Adventurers*. This is also a form of pastoral care (see Appendix C).

Sunday School teachers can also be encouraged to have a Saturday outing with their children in the summer months or to organize a 'Holiday Club' in one of the school holidays (see Appendix C). Both these activities can very easily involve the whole family, and this has many advantages not only for keeping control but for the cementing of friendships made at the Sunday services.

Crèche
If there is a rota of women looking after the weekly crèche perhaps they might be prepared also to visit the homes of their babies. However, it may well be that these have been contacted initially in connection with Baptism, and therefore the vicar or assistant curate may be more suitable to deal with them.

2 Integrating new families into the church
Family Worship will have failed in its purpose if it is not producing *active* Christian disciples. We must therefore give careful consideration as to how we integrate the Family Service congregation with the other congregation in our church. We need constantly to be on our guard that the Family Service does not give rise to two entirely separate congregations sharing one building, and the adults of the Family Service never getting any spiritual nourishment beyond what is suitable for 12-year-olds. Basically there are three ways in which the parochial programme should cater for those outsiders reached through Family Service, to help them become insiders.

1 Worship
In the past there has been a tendency, certainly in evangelical circles of the Church of England, for there to be a considerable over-catering for one group. The pattern of services on a Sunday has usually been: Holy Communion at 8, Morning Prayer at 11 and Evening Prayer at 6.30. During the week there has been a midweek Bible study and prayer meeting. If one noted who actually came to these services, one would find that, generally speaking, they were the same people-people who have been coming to these activities for years. The effect has been that the parson has had to spend a considerable amount of time preparing original sermons and Bible studies for the same audience

year after year, to the almost total neglect of a vast number of people in his parish, with the result that spiritually the few are grossly overfed while all around thousands are dying of hunger.

There should be provision for everyone in the parish to be able to worship at least once according to his or her own degree of spiritual enlightenment. We often hear the complaint that the sermon was either far too complicated or that it didn't say anything that wasn't known already. Yet when a preacher is confronted with a congregation consisting perhaps of children, parents who have only just resumed church attendance since Sunday School days, and some people in the congregation who have been coming to church for years and may even be committee members of important Christian organizations, the sermon can hardly have an adequate message for everyone.

The Bible recognizes that some people need the plain facts of the gospel because they are not yet converted. 'For I decided to know nothing among you, except Jesus Christ, and him crucified' (1 Corinthians 2.2). Those young in the faith need the sincere milk of the Word, whereas others are ready for strong meat. 'Like newborn babes, long for the pure spiritual milk, that by it you may grow up to salvation' (1 Peter 2.2); 'I fed you with milk, not solid food; for you were not ready for it; and even yet you are not ready' (1 Corinthians 3.2); 'For everyone who lives on milk is unskilled in the word of righteousness, for he is a child. But solid food is for the mature, for those who have their faculties trained by practice to distinguish good from evil' (Hebrews 5.13–14). It is unreasonable to expect even the most accomplished preacher to include such a variation of diet in one meal.

The way to overcome this may well be All-age Instruction, as considered in chapter 4.

Apart then from the weekly Family Service, there should be a weekly gathering together of the church to break bread. Of all our Sunday services, the Holy Communion is surely the most important. This is the one service our Lord especially commanded should take place. It obviously had a very prominent place in the life of the early church, and was probably celebrated weekly. Holy Communion or the Lord's Supper, as its name implies, is an occasion for fellowship in which Christians have communion with Jesus Christ and with one another. It therefore seems logical that it should be held when most people can come together. Yet, sadly, it is often celebrated when least people can come. The Communion Service is one of the two occasions referred to in our Prayer Book when there should be a ministry of the Word, and I believe this should mean a proper exposition of Scripture and instruction in biblical doctrine for Christian believers. I have even used the sermon time at Holy Communion for a course in evangelism for lay parish workers with duplicated notes provided. It is therefore advisable to hold it later than 8 am.

We must therefore make provision for parents who have grown spiritually beyond Family Service (though they may still come) to be able to attend Holy Communion. One way of doing this is that suggested in chapter 4. In some situations it may be necessary for older married Christians to look after children (say once a month) while parents attend the sacrament.

Hugh Pruen in an article in the *Church Times*[1] about Parish Communion refers to some warnings from the former Archbishop of Canterbury in the 1950s:[2]

'First, the lack of teaching and understanding which could mean that the Parish Communion could become little more than a weekly and rather meaningless habit in the same way that other acts of worship can so easily do. Secondly, and following from this, the disregard by individuals of Communion as a responsible and awe-inspiring personal act. And lastly, a superficial idea of fellowship.'

In our own Family Worship we would all no doubt be wise to take these warnings to heart and take the spiritual temperature from time to time.

Some family worshippers may begin to attend Evening Prayer. We need to make sure then that these services have been updated, the language modernized, lively singing encouraged and visual aids perhaps sometimes used in the presentation of the sermon. In this television age, people of all ages are so used to learning visually that surely the church should not be out of date in this respect. I have found soundstrips and even blackboard and chalk illustrations perfectly acceptable to an adult congregation.[3]

2   Fellowship

There should be some meetings for fellowship for different groups of people according to age and circumstances. The great emphasis in the New Testament was on the fellowship that Christians enjoyed with one another. Christians were not to forsake the gathering of

[1] 4 October 1974.
[2] Michael Ramsey, *Durham Essays and Addresses.*
[3] See further, Michael Botting, *Evangelistic Services* (Grove Booklets on Ministry and Worship, no. 21), especially chapter 5.

themselves together (Hebrews 10.24–25). Such fellowship provoked to love and good works; therefore provision must be made in a church's programme or it is unscriptural, although the parson should not always be expected to be present, or he will never have any time for evening visiting.

In my previous parish we developed a system which, although it made no claims to particular originality, was suited to our needs. Normally on the first Wednesday of each month, we held what we called the Church Fellowship, to which all sections of the church were expected to come. No other church activities were held that week. I planned the programme at this meeting, which usually included a short Bible study on some topical issue, a special item such as a short film or talk, time to discuss any matters affecting the local church where I wanted to sound wider opinion than the Parochial Church Council, and ending with some time for corporate prayer.

On the other weeks of the month, House Bible Studies were held in a number of homes in the parish, as widely spread out as possible. These were led by lay people and catered for different physical and spiritual age groups. The leaders of the groups met with me from time to time to plan the Bible studies, and kept me in touch with the problems of those attending. It was intended that these house groups should be places where members of the church really could share and so bear one another's burdens (see Galatians 6.2).

Those familiar with the work of 'Alcoholics Anonymous' or 'Gamblers Anonymous' will know that members in presenting a testimony begin by stating that they are compulsive drinkers or gamblers, and then proceed to tell their story. It can be a tremendous encouragement to others present to hear this open confession and to know that there are others like themselves, who have managed to keep off drink or gambling for some time. Surely we in the church fellowship should be able to have the humility and, in so many words, to be able to stand up in a group and say, 'I am a compulsive sinner but . . .', and so provoke each other to love and good works. How often it seems that when Christians gather together they can become criticizing centres to which one would never dare introduce a new Christian who may not yet have grown out of his or her non-Christian behaviour.

All this is tremendously relevant to the subject of Family Services, for if we are going to bring families into the church, and keep them, we must also have a warm fellowship to which they can be introduced. The monthly church fellowship and the house Bible study groups have an important role to play in this respect, as do also our young wives groups, men's fellowship and, better still, any developments of fellowship for all the family such as we have been discussing in chapter 6.

3 Service

The service of God in the world is to be executed by all Christian people and it is the particular task of those in the ordained ministry to prepare the laity for their work of witness to the world (see Ephesians 4.11–12 NEB, 1 Peter 2.9–10). This may occasionally be hinted at in Family Service talks, stated quite explicitly in Confirmation preparation, and positively encouraged by a personal visit by the clergy when a suitable job in the parish needs doing that one of the new Family Service members could reasonably be expected to do. The more we make them feel they are indispensable, the more chance we have of retaining them in our congregation.

There may be occasions when an adult converted through Family Service might be asked to give a word of public testimony, say at Family Service itself or at Evening Prayer, perhaps to illustrate a point during the sermon.

If the parish publishes a magazine or newssheet, a written testimony may well be valuable, not only for the person writing it but also for outsiders who may read it. An occasional visitor to a Family Service was talking to someone she met in the park when they were both out with their babies, when she suddenly discovered that this person was none other than the person who had written her testimony in the magazine. This brought home to her the reality of the Christian faith in everyday life, and she became a confirmed and regular member of the congregation.

In due course the family may be able to have a real share in the evangelizing of other families, in the ways suggested in chapter 7. Indeed, who better to use than those who have been won for Christ because the local church has 'thought family'.

The Report *Towards the Conversion of England* states:

'It is the *presentation* of the gospel, not its *content*, that changes with succeeding generations and their varying conditions. We have so to present Christ Jesus that the people of our particular age may come to accept Him as Saviour and King. This calls for a presentation expressed in terms and images consonant with present day thinking and experience.'[1]

This means that it is vitally important to make sure that our services and meetings are always geared to the needs of our parochial situation. We believe that the strategy for our time is one that attempts to reach the whole family as a unit. It was gratifying, therefore, that the Chairman at the National Study Week at Morecambe on 'Strategy for Evangelism' (the Rev. John Stott) in his summing-up should include among his main points, 'The need to concentrate on homes and families'. The late Alan Stibbs, one-time CIM missionary and latterly Vice-Principal of Oak Hill Theological College, is quoted as saying, 'in missionary strategy the primary unit to be laboured with is the family'. But this thinking is no longer merely theoretical. Throughout the country wherever churches are trying this biblical method of approach they are finding that God is giving the increase and adding to their number those who are being saved.

[1] *Towards the Conversion of England*: The Report of a Commission on Evangelism appointed by the Archbishops of Canterbury and York in memory of the late Archbishop William Temple, page 17.

Appendix A An Order of Service for Family Worship

INTRODUCTION

All stand (*The following or other words from the Bible may be used by the Minister*).

Minister

Come close to God, and he will come close to you.   (James 4.8 NEB)
The Lord our God is worthy to receive glory and honour and power for he has created and redeemed us.

Minister and People together

Heavenly Father, in our worship help us to sing your praise, confess our sins, hear your Word and bring our prayers to you, through Jesus Christ our Lord.   Amen.

HYMN

CONFESSION

either   or

Minister	*Minister*
If we say we have no sin we deceive ourselves and the truth is not in us.	I will arise and go to my Father and will say to him.
People	*People*
If we confess our sins God is faithful and just to forgive us our sins and to cleanse us from every kind of wrong. (cf. 1 John 1.8–9)	Father, I have sinned against heaven and before you and am no more worthy to be called your son. (cf. Luke 15.18–19)

Minister

Let us confess our sins to God.

Minister and People together

Almighty God, we confess that we have sinned against you in thought, word and deed: we have not loved you with all our heart; we have not loved our neighbours as ourselves. Have mercy upon us: cleanse us from our sins; and help us to overcome our faults: through Jesus Christ our Lord.   Amen.

Either the following prayer or an alternative:

Minister

May God, our heavenly Father, who has promised to forgive all those who sincerely turn to him, have mercy on each one of you, deliver you from your sins, and strengthen you for his service: through Jesus Christ our Lord.   Amen.

PRAISE

Minister
Let us praise God for his mercy.
People
And give thanks to him for his goodness.
Minister
Open our lips, O Lord.
People
And our mouths shall declare your praise.

All stand

PSALM, CANTICLE OR HYMN

If a Psalm or Canticle is used end with:
Glory to the Father, and ' to the ' Son: and ' to the ' Holy ' Spirit; as in the be ' ginning, so ' now : and for ' ever. ' A'men.

All sit for a reading from the Bible

(*This may be followed by a special activity.*)

CANTICLE, HYMN OR CHORUSES

(*Another reading from the Bible followed by a hymn or canticle may be included here. The Talk may also be given at this part of the Service, if preferred.*)

BELIEF
All stand

either | or

Minister
Do you believe in God?
People
I believe in God the Father who made me and all the world.
Minister
Do you believe in Jesus Christ?
People
I believe in Jesus Christ, the Son of God, who came to this earth to be my Saviour. He died for my sins on the cross, rose again from the dead, ascended to the Father in heaven and will come again in his glory as the Judge of all people.
Minister
Do you believe in the Holy Spirit?

Minister and People shall say together the Apostles' Creed:
I believe in God the Father almighty, Creator of heaven and earth.
I believe in Jesus Christ, his only Son, our Lord.
He was conceived by the power of the Holy Spirit
and born of the Virgin Mary,
He suffered under Pontius Pilate,
was crucified, died, and was buried.
He descended to the dead.
On the third day he rose again.
He ascended into heaven,
and is seated at the right hand of the Father.

People
I believe in the Holy Spirit, whom God gives to all who trust in Christ. He makes me more like Jesus, guides and strengthens me in my daily life, and helps me to serve God in the family of the Church.

He will come again to judge the living and the dead.
I believe in the Holy Spirit,
the holy catholic Church,
the communion of saints,
the forgiveness of sins,
the resurrection of the body,
and the life everlasting.

Minister
May Almighty God strengthen this faith in us.
Let us pray.

PRAYER

The Lord's Prayer
Our Father in heaven,
Hallowed be your Name,
your kingdom come,
your will be done,
on earth as in heaven.
Give us today our daily bread.
Forgive us our sins
as we forgive those who sin against us.
Do not bring us to the time of trial
but deliver us from evil.
For the kingdom, the power and the glory are yours
now and for ever.   Amen.

The special Prayer of the Day

A Prayer for the Queen and all in Authority
Almighty God, our Heavenly Father, we pray for our Queen and the Royal Family, the members of Parliament and all in authority; that they may govern our country with wisdom and understanding and for the good of your Church and all people, through Jesus Christ our Lord.   Amen.

A Prayer for our families and homes to be said together
Heavenly Father, we thank you for our homes and families, for our food and clothing and for all the happiness that parents and children can share. We ask that your love may surround us, your care may protect us, and that we may know your peace at all times, for Jesus' sake.   Amen.

HYMN

THE TALK

HYMN

Minister
Let us say together:

Be with us, Lord, as we go out into the world. May the lips that have sung your praises always speak the truth; may the ears which have heard your Word listen only to what is good and may our lives as well as our worship be always pleasing in your sight, for the glory of Jesus Christ our Lord.   Amen.

THE BLESSING

or

The Grace of our Lord Jesus Christ, and the love of God, and the fellowship of the Holy Spirit be with us all evermore.   Amen.

Appendix B A three-year plan

3-year syllabus for use at Family Service and all-age instruction

(from the first Sunday in September to the last Sunday in August)

1 The Creation
2 The Fall
3 Cain and Abel
4 Noah
5 The Flood
6 Harvest (based on Genesis 8.22)
7 Babel
8 The Call of Abraham
9 Lot
10 Sodom and Gomorrah
11 The Birth of Isaac
12 A Bride for Isaac
13 Jacob and Esau
14 An Advent Talk (selected from Matthew 24 and 25)
15 A Bible Sunday Talk
16 An Old Testament Prophecy about the Coming of Jesus
17 Christmas Tree Service–'The Name of Jesus' (Matthew 1.18–25)
18 Christmas Day–The Wise Men
19 The Holy Innocents (Matthew 2.13–23)
20 'A Blessed New Year' (New Year Talk based on the Beatitudes, Matthew 5)
21 Jesus the Teacher (Matthew 5–7)
22 Jesus the Healer (Matthew 8)
23 The Call of the Disciples (Matthew 10)
24 Jesus and the Sabbath (Matthew 12)
25 The Parable of the Sower (Matthew 13)
26 The Feeding of the Five Thousand (Matthew 14)
27 Peter's Recognition of Jesus at Caesarea Philippi (Matthew 16)
28 The Transfiguration (Matthew 17)
29 Mothering Sunday (based on teaching from Matthew 18 and 19)
30 The Rich Young Ruler or the Labourers in the Vineyard (Matthew 19 or 20)
31 The Entry into Jerusalem (Palm Sunday–based on Matthew 21)
32 Good Friday (talk based on the Passion according to Matthew)
33 Easter Day (the Resurrection according to Matthew 28.1–15)
34 The Great Commissioning (Missionary talk based on Matthew 28.16–20)
35 Joseph the Dreamer sold into Egypt
36 Joseph–a slave in Egypt
37 Joseph–a prince in Egypt
38 Joseph Reveals Himself to his Brothers
39 Israel comes to Egypt
40 A Whitsunday Talk

90 Easter Day, according to Luke (Suggestion: the Walk to Emmaus)
91 Jesus Appears in the Upper Room
92 Ruth and Naomi
93 Ruth and Boaz
94 Hannah
95 Samuel as a Boy
96 The Ascension (Acts 1)
97 Pentecost (Acts 2)
98 The Healing of the Lame Man (Acts 3 and 4)
99 Ananias and Sapphira (Acts 5)
100 The Appointment of the Deacons (Acts 6)
101 Philip (Acts 8)
102 The Conversion of Saul (Acts 9)
103 Peter's Vision and the Opening of the Door to the Gentiles (Acts 10 and 11)
104 The Death of James, and Peter Released from Prison (Acts 12)
105 Holiday Series on the Lord's Prayer (Luke 11)—'Our Father'
106 'Your will be done'
107 'Give us . . . '
108 'Forgive us . . . '
109 'Lead us not . . . ' (or, 'do not bring us . . . ')
110 Samuel the Prophet
111 Saul made King
112 Saul's Disobedience
113 The Anointing and Commissioning of David
114 The Wheat and the Tares (Harvest talk based on Matthew 13)
115 David and Goliath
116 David and Jonathan
117 David and Saul
118 David made King
119 David and Bathsheba
120 David and Absalom
121 Solomon
122 An Advent Talk (possibly based on the Epistles to the Thessalonians)
123 Bible Sunday—Jeremiah and the Scroll
124 Jesus—the Word of God
125 Jesus—the Lamb of God
126 Christmas Day—The Appearance of the Angels to the Shepherds (Luke 2.8–20)
127 Stephen (Acts 6 and 7)
128 Peter and Andrew (John 1.35–42)
129 Jesus and Nathaniel (John 1.43–51)
130 The Wedding Feast at Cana (John 2.1–11)
131 Jesus and the Money-changers (John 2.13–22)
132 Nicodemus (John 3)

Though originally prepared for *Reaching the Families* (revised), this Syllabus also appears in *Christian Education on Sunday mornings*, ed. C. H. Hutchins (Grove Booklet No. 31).

Appendix C Books, aids and equipment

General

Peter R. Akehurst, *Community, prayer and the individual* (Grove booklet on ministry and worship, No. 18)

John Benington, *Culture, class and Christian belief* (Scripture Union, 1973)

Michael Botting, *Evangelistic services, their value and limitations* (Grove booklet on ministry and worship, No. 21)

Bernard Braley, Maintenance and equipment news (Vol. 11, No. 1, 1969), *The baby and the bath water*, an article on changes in Christian worship

Colin O. Buchanan, *Patterns of Sunday worship* (Grove booklet on ministry and worship, no. 9)

Beryl Bye, *A Christian's guide to teaching our children the Christian faith* (Hodder & Stoughton, 1965)

Ralph Capenerhurst, *You in your small corner* (IVP)

Anthony and Elizabeth Capon, *The Church and the child* (Hodder and Stoughton, 1967)

Larry Christensen, *The Christian family* (Fountain Trust, 1971)

E. W. Crabb, *Train up a child* (Paternoster Press, 1954)

Guy Daniel, *The enemy is boredom* (Darton, Longman & Todd, 1964). Includes collects in modern English.

Lewis A. Drummond, *Evangelism: The counter revolution* (Marshall, Morgan and Scott)

Leslie Earnshaw, *Worship for the seventies* (Denholm House Press, 1973)

Donald English, *Evangelism and worship* (Methodist Church Home Mission Department)

Richard Hoggart, *The uses of literacy* (Pelican, 1957)

Erroll Hulse (ed.), *Reformation for the family* (Henry E. Walter)

Mary Alice Jones, *Parents, children and the Christian faith* (Fontana, 1967)

Trevor Lloyd, *Informal liturgy* (Grove booklet on ministry and worship, no. 6)

Martyn D. Lloyd-Jones, *Life in the Spirit in marriage, home and work* (Banner of Truth, 1974)

Keith Miller, *The taste of new wine* (especially chapter 4) (Word)

Margaret V. Old, *Today's children, tomorrow's Church* (Scripture Union, 1974)

Martin Parsons, *Family life* (Falcon, 1972)

J. A. Petersen (ed.), *The marriage affair*—(The family counsellor)

Gavin Reid, *The gagging of God* (Hodder and Stoughton)

Ivan Reid, *Sunday Schools for the seventies*

Ivan Reid, *A survey of ten Sunday Schools in the Leeds District of the Methodist Church* (write to Mr Reid, University of Bradford, BD7 1DP, Yorkshire)

Alan Stibbs, *Family life today* (Marcham Manor Press)

John Tanburn, *Open house* (Falcon)

J. P. Taylor and others, *Evangelism among children and young people* (Scripture Union, 1967)

Margaret Warde, *Take my home* (Scripture Union, 1969)

Douglas Webster, *Yes to mission* (SCM Press, 1966)

John Wilkinson, *Family and evangelistic services* (Church Information Office, 1967)

Susan Williams, *Lord of our world* (Falcon)—modern collects

M. A. P. Wood, *Like a mighty army* (Marshall, Morgan and Scott, 1955)

On the other side (The report of the Evangelical Alliance Commission on Evangelism—Scripture Union)

Prayers we have in common (The International Consultation on English Texts—Geoffrey Chapman, 1970)

Together in church (Methodist Youth Department, 2 Chester House, Pages Lane, London N10 1PZ)

Tools for evangelism (from the National Study Week at Morecambe on 'Strategy for evangelism'—Church Book Room Press)

Towards the conversion of England (A report of a Commission on Evangelism appointed by the Archbishops of Canterbury and York. Press and Publications Board of the Church Assembly, 1945)

Books on preparation of sermons

M. H. Botting, *Teaching the families* (Falcon, 1973)

A. C. Capon, *Know how to give a children's talk* (Scripture Union, 1963)

J. W. Harmer, *The scripture lesson* (IVF, 1945)

J. R. Hill and G. R. Harding Wood, *God and the children* (Paternoster Press, 1936)

R. Hudson Pope, *To teach others also* (CSSM, 1953)

Jean James, *Primary teaching in Sunday Schools* (Scripture Union, 1959)

Guy King and others, *Sunday School lesson books* 1–6

Peter W. Liddelow, *Know how to use audio and visual aids* (Scripture Union, 1963)

Martyn D. Lloyd-Jones, *Preaching and preachers* (Hodder and Stoughton, 1971)

Margaret V. Old, *Know how to run children's holiday clubs* (Scripture Union, 1965)

W. E. Sangster, *The craft of sermon construction* (Epworth Press, 1949)

C. W. Woods, *Communication* (A privately duplicated booklet available from the Vicarage, 1 Lower Oxford Road, Basford, Newcastle, Staffs.)

Teaching publications

Gospel Light: total Bible teaching plan, full details from Gospel Light Publications, 27 Camden Road, London NW1.

Scripture Press Sunday School curriculum: all Bible graded series, available from Scripture Press Foundation (UK) Ltd., 372 Caledonian Road, London N1.

Scripture Union teaching materials for beginners, primaries, juniors and teenagers, with take-home leaflets for all ages: Scripture Union, 5 Wigmore Street, London W1.

Books relating to Baptism and Confirmation

Baptism and Confirmation, a report submitted by the Church of England Liturgical Commission to the Archbishops of Canterbury and York (SPCK, 1966)

Colin Buchanan, *Baptismal discipline* (Grove booklet no. 3)

Colin Buchanan, *A case for Infant Baptism* (Grove booklet no. 20)

Christopher Bycroft, *A service of thanksgiving and blessing* (Grove booklet no. 5)

Christopher Bycroft, *Communion, Confirmation and commitment* (Grove booklet no. 8)

Frank Colquhoun, *Your child's Baptism* (Hodder and Stoughton, 1958)

R. H. Green, *A time for decision* (from the Diocese of London Youth Service, St Andrew's, St Andrew Street, London EC4)

Geoffrey Hart, *Right to baptize*, The contemporary dilemma (Hodder and Stoughton—Christian Foundation Series no. 14, 1966)

Joachim Jeremias, *Infant Baptism in the first four centuries* (SCM Press, 1960)

Pierre Ch. Marcel, *The biblical doctrine of Infant Baptism* (James Clark & Co., translation, 1953)

J. A. Motyer, *Baptism in the Book of Common Prayer* (FEC Publications, 1961)

Services of Baptism and Confirmation (Marcham Manor Press, Latimer monograph no. 2, 1967)

J. R. W. Stott, *The evangelical doctrine of Baptism* in *The Anglican synthesis* (ed. W. R. F. Browning Smith, 1964)

J. Stafford Wright, *The child's right to Baptism* (Church Book Room Press, 1951)

Audio and visual aids, etc.

Many suggestions can be found in:

Audio-visual media: A guide to sources of material, by Stephen Travis. (Grove booklet no. 6)

AVA magazine (50p p.a. from Edinburgh House, 2 Eaton Gate, London SW1; quarterly magazine with useful AVA reviews)
Teaching the families (particularly section 1) ed. M. H. Botting (Falcon, 1973)

Other suggestions and sources for audio-visual aid materials, equipment, filmstrips, etc.:
Church Pastoral Aid Society, Falcon Court, 32 Fleet Street, London EC4Y 1DB.
Filmstrips, soundstrips, Group Learning Courses; AVA hire.
Church Army Filmstrip Hire Dept., 185 Marylebone Road, London NW1 5QL.
Comprehensive catalogue available at small cost.
Concordia, 117–123 Golden Lane, London EC1.
Filmstrips, projectors, films.
Gospel Sound and Vision, 44 Georgia Road, Thornton Heath, Surrey, CR4 8DW (01–764 1520)
Scripture Union AVA Dept., Brunel House, St George Road, Bristol BS1 5XB.
Wide selection of filmstrips for sale and hire, including some on how to teach children.
SPCK AVA Centre, 29 Tufton Street, London SW1.
Filmstrips and equipment.
Clear Vue Projection Company, 92 Stroud Green Road, London N4.
Filmstrips, screens and projectors.
E. J. Arnold and Co. Ltd., Visual Department, Butterly Street, Leeds 10. Teazlegraph cloth and stickers (Teazlegraph material is marketed in two colours (blue and grey), width 42″ and sold by the yard (approx. £2 at the time of going to print). Only available by post unless you live in Leeds, and needs to be ordered.)
Church Youth Fellowship Association, Falcon Court, 32 Fleet Street, London EC4Y 1DB
Soundstrips.
Matthews, Drew and Shelbourne Ltd., The Visual Aids Centre, 78 High Holborn, London WC1.
A very useful visual aids catalogue, which is free when in stock.
Christian Literature Crusade, The Dean, Alresford, Hants (and shops). Useful catalogue including filmstrips, AVA equipment and Sunday School materials.
The Rev. A. Beck, Puritan Vicarage, Bridgwater, Somerset.
35 mm. slides available for a small charge to cover cost.
The Econasign Co. Ltd., 19–21 Palace Street, London SW1.
Lettering outfits and Fluorcard and paper in 5 colours—red, yellow, orange, green and magenta. The 4″ stencil outfit is especially valuable. The initial outlay to purchase these may seem rather exorbitant, but those speaking frequently to large groups need to be able to produce clear lettering of a high standard, and the saving of time will considerably compensate for the price.

Grampian Reproducers Ltd., Hanworth Trading Estate, Feltham, Middx.
Grampian neck cord (for holding halter microphone).
Vision Screen Services Ltd., Riversdale House, North Fambridge, Chelmsford, Essex.
Overhead projector and materials, etc.

Music etc.

Family worship (words only) CPAS—revised edition, 1975
Hymns of faith (music and words) Scripture Union
Psalm praise (music and words) Falcon 1973
A New Testament Psalter St Mary's Church, Woodford, Essex, 1963
Scripture Union choruses (music and words) Scripture Union
Youth praise 1 *and* 2 (music and words) Falcon
Sing to God (music and words) Scripture Union
Come and sing (music edition only) Scripture Union

Ideas for improving Confirmation courses

Believing and belonging—a Group learning course in 12 parts to introduce adults and older young people to church membership and the Christian faith. Includes group discussion material, soundstrips, taped interviews, wall charts, etc. Available from CPAS.

Your Confirmation, John Stott (Hodder and Stoughton, 1958). Also set of six soundstrips of the same title, illustrated by Gordon Stowell (from CPAS)
Into membership, Richard Gorrie (Falcon, 1968)

Filmstrips available on hire from Scripture Union, Brunel House, St George's Road, Bristol, BS1 5XB

Head in the sand (with tape), to encourage personal Bible reading.
Hit or miss (with tape), a Christian attitude to money.
RE In schools series: particularly
Worship
Relationships
Living in society

Filmstrips available on hire from CPAS, Falcon Court, 32 Fleet Street, London, EC4Y 1DB.

What is a missionary? (with tape) to encourage Christian service.
What is a man? (soundstrip) evangelistic
Baptism (soundstrip) infant baptism
The Jesus meal (soundstrip) soundstrip on Series 3 Communion.

FAMILY WORSHIP

You have read how to reach the families and are now wondering about building your services. *Family Worship* can provide some answers to the questions in your mind. It is a book based on the experiences of Michael Botting and others who have embarked on this venture before you and is geared to the person who is not familiar with a prayer book and the other trappings of formal worship.

This revised edition contains a selection of hymns, psalms and prayers as well as orders of worship for a family service, Baptism, Mothering Sunday and Harvest. It aims to include all the material needed for a service in one easy-to-handle book.

Prayers for Today's Church

For some years people have felt that a selection of prayers was needed to supplement the *Book of Common Prayer*. Where was the hard-pressed clergyman to turn for a litany on education? Where would he find a thanksgiving for man's achievements in science and outer space? Dick Williams has gathered together prayers on these and many other subjects, both modern and timeless, local and universal, which go a long way to meet the needs of our expanding world.

This book, which is not geared to any specific denomination, includes sections on the Christian year and experimental forms of worship. It can be used effectively in congregational worship and for family prayers at home.

A best seller since its publication in 1966, *Youth Praise* offers a collection of modern hymns, drawn from a great variety of sources and covering a wide spectrum of tastes. It includes songs and choruses which can be sung joyfully by congregations and youth groups as well as more meditative solo items. Michael Baughen edits the two volumes which make up *Youth Praise*, and among other contributors are Michael Saward, Timothy Dudley-Smith and Richard Bewes.

The books are available in a words only edition as well as one containing both words and music.

PSALM PRAISE

This collection of lively tunes proves that psalm singing need no longer be a dirge-like and embarrassing part of a service. It presents its material in many different and interesting ways. There are both chants and spirited tunes. For the person who enjoys the majesty of 17th century English, there are psalms and portions of scripture in their familiar Prayer Book form, whilst other people, who might wish to worship in modern language, will find hymns and poems based on biblical passages. The contributors include Timothy Dudley-Smith, Christopher Idle, Norman Warren and Michael Baughen, who edited the book.

This book would be a great asset to those contemplating beginning family services.